T0248104

# THE
# POWER OF
# SCARCITY

# THE
# POWER OF
# SCARCITY

## LEVERAGING URGENCY AND DEMAND
## TO INFLUENCE CUSTOMER DECISIONS

MINDY WEINSTEIN, PhD

NEW YORK    CHICAGO    SAN FRANCISCO    ATHENS    LONDON
MADRID    MEXICO CITY    MILAN    NEW DELHI
SINGAPORE    SYDNEY    TORONTO

1  2  3  4  5  6  7  8  9    LCR    27  26  25  24  23  22

ISBN        978-1-264-27823-7
MHID        1-264-27823-3

e-ISBN      978-1-264-27824-4
e-MHID      1-264-27824-1

**Library of Congress Cataloging-in-Publication Data**

Names: Weinstein, Mindy, author.
Title: The power of scarcity : leveraging urgency and demand to influence customer decisions / Mindy Weinstein.
Description: New York : McGraw Hill, [2023] | Includes bibliographical references and index.
Identifiers: LCCN 2022028165 | ISBN 9781264278237 (hardback) | ISBN 9781264278244 (ebook)
Subjects: LCSH: Scarcity. | Supply and demand. | Consumer behavior.
Classification: LCC HB801.W45 2023 | DDC 338.5/21—dc23/eng/ 20220623
LC record available at https://lccn.loc.gov/2022028165

McGraw Hill books are available at special quantity discounts to use as premiums and sales promotions or for use in corporate training programs. To contact a representative, please visit the Contact Us pages at www.mhprofessional.com.

McGraw Hill is committed to making our products accessible to all learners. To learn more about the available support and accommodations we offer, please contact us at accessibility@mheducation.com. We also participate in the Access Text Network (www.accesstext.org), and ATN members may submit requests through ATN.

To my husband, Mike, and my two boys, Quentin and Bryson, who make me laugh and smile every day.

# Contents

# PART TWO
## USING SCARCITY

# Introduction

IT MIGHT SOUND MELODRAMATIC to say that everything changed that day in 2017. It was another 110-degree day in Phoenix, literally hot enough to fry an egg on the sidewalk. The heat didn't get to me that morning, though, because I had a meeting with renowned social psychologist Robert Cialdini. Dr. Cialdini had graciously agreed to meet with me to discuss an academic topic, but our conversation became so much more. Over a cup of coffee, we discussed persuasion and its powerful psychological impact. We talked about the subtle ways wording a message can lead to greater influence. We even talked about FOMO (fear of missing out) and the havoc it wreaks on the mind.

That one-hour conversation led me on a three-year journey into researching, experimenting with, and understanding scarcity.

It's no secret that scarcity can lead to tunnel vision. People become consumed with what they can't or don't have—which is why marketers often use scarcity messages in their campaigns.

But there is so much more to scarcity than simple supply and demand. It's not as simple as, if we think something is scarce, we'll want it more. There are many more layers of complexity involved that can tip the scales on whether scarcity will prompt someone to take action or walk away.

In other words, scarcity isn't straightforward, and using it the wrong way can backfire. Let's look at two examples of scarcity, one recent and one classic.

## THE PANDEMIC AND THE RUN ON TOILET PAPER

As the worldwide Covid-19 pandemic quickly spread, consumers began stocking up on toilet paper and clearing out store inventories. It was not uncommon to see empty shelves, as retailers struggled to keep stocked with the now-hot commodity.

People became obsessed with getting their hands on toilet paper—because obsession is a classic side effect of scarcity. The lower the inventories of toilet paper became, the more obsessed people were with getting their hands on it. Toilet paper became nearly impossible to find at local stores, and those stores couldn't get enough product from their distributors, even though distributors were getting their normal supply from manufacturers. Demand skyrocketed. Fights between customers erupted in stores, some so heated that police were called in to intervene.

The sudden toilet paper crisis baffled economists and researchers—it wasn't just a national problem; it was a global problem. A café in Australia started accepting rolls of toilet paper as payment. The price of that cup of coffee you wanted? Three rolls. Armed robbers in Hong Kong raided a local supermarket and took 600 rolls of toilet paper, but nothing else.

One of the prevailing theories regarding the sudden run on toilet paper is that people were afraid there wouldn't be any when they needed it. Toilet paper was perceived as a scarce resource sparking immense competition among consumers trying to purchase it.

## TICKLE ME ELMO

Twenty-four years earlier, a different shortage—albeit no less unusual—occurred involving a talking Sesame Street toy.

> The internet buzzes with rumors of toy-store cashiers trampled by Elmo-crazed crowds, of Elmos being scalped for $7,000 apiece. Newspaper classified columns bulge with ads asking $1,000 for Elmo, which retails for $29.99 and is the most hard-to-find holiday toy since the Cabbage Patch Doll of 1983. Even the Mafia has joined the frenzy.
>
> *NEW YORK TIMES,* 1996[1]

If you were a child, parent, or grandparent in the mid-1990s, you probably remember the Tickle Me Elmo craze that swept the nation. The 16-inch *Sesame Street* figure, which laughed and said, "That tickles!" when its belly was squeezed, caused mass chaos during the Christmas season of 1996. Tyco Toys Inc., the manufacturer of Tickle Me Elmo, expected moderate success of its toy during Christmas; Tyco certainly did not anticipate what actually happened.

Tickle Me Elmo was featured on Rosie O'Donnell's television show and promoted in ads on television as the holiday season approached. Just one day after Thanksgiving, nearly 800,000 Elmo dolls—Tyco's entire inventory—had been snapped up within hours. What happened next? News spread about the Elmo doll shortage, which only increased the demand for it—and gave rise to the hysteria that followed. Parents became obsessed with getting the toy for their children. As the *New York Times* reported, some were even willing to pay $7,000 for the $29.99 toy.

---

Although the Tickle Me Elmo and toilet paper examples are vastly different, they share a common theme—scarcity. Products and services can become scarce for a variety of reasons; it is not always a simple economic dilemma of supply and demand. Limited-time offers and products, limited editions, and low supply and high demand are all forms of scarcity and lead to limited availability. Specifically, scarcity falls into these categories:

- **Supply-related scarcity.** This form of scarcity occurs when there are not that many products available due to a shortage and is often reflected in such phrases as "supplies are limited," and "while supplies last."

- **Limited-edition scarcity.** This is a version of supply-related scarcity. A limited edition is based on the limited number of units produced and is typically a slightly modified version of the original.

- **Time-related scarcity.** This type of scarcity derives from a product promotion, limited availability, or level of supply during an allotted window of time. The time restriction results in scarcity.

- **Demand-related scarcity.** This form of scarcity is defined
  as a shortage resulting from popularity and high demand.
  In other words, the demand exceeds the product's supply.
  Demand-related scarcity is often indicated by such
  phrases as "[#] units sold" or "only [#] left" and "nearly
  sold out due to high demand."

You can find these same terms in the "Scarcity Definitions at a
Glance" section at the back of the book on page 187 for quick
reference.

Our ancestors competed over scare resources, and in modern society, we still do the same. However, this time we are not
generally competing over survival items, but instead for products
and services that have limited availability. Take NFTs (nonfun-
gible tokens) as an example. NFTs, which can be anything from
drawings to music to AI, were considered valuable because of
the inherent uniqueness and scarcity. Scarcity was driving up the
value and price people were willing to pay. For instance, one NFT
sold for $69 million.[2]

Apparently, people haven't changed much since the dawn of
humankind.

## THE POWER OF SCARCITY

Scarcity is a rarely discussed but incredibly powerful principle.
When applied correctly, it can boost sales, win negotiations,
ignite action, develop community, build customer loyalty, and
create fun and excitement. Scarcity has been identified as one of
several principles of influence. And out of all the influence principles, scarcity is one of the most powerful because it invokes

primal instincts that are key to survival. Our ancestors had to survive when scarcity was prevalent. While we might not need to hunt and gather scarce resources like our ancestors did, that instinct hasn't gone away. We still experience the feeling of loss and regret if we don't get our hands on a scarce product or service. The urgency to take action becomes overwhelming.

This book is all about the concept of scarcity, but not from an economic point of view. Yes, scarcity is at the heart of economics: the principle of supply and demand. Scarcity also exists in the world of psychology, and it is a reason behind many of the purchases we make. It is also the catalyst for increased sales for businesses, and thus higher revenues. If used correctly, scarcity can influence the people who use your products or services.

The idea of influencing others has always fascinated me. Not in the "I want to manipulate you" kind of way—scarcity has to be used ethically—but in a way so I could deeply understand why certain words or circumstances persuade people to act. For instance, why did someone buy yet another TV, laptop, smartphone, pair of sunglasses, pair of shoes, bottle of wine, or . . . (fill in the blank) when he or she didn't really need it? Could it have been that it was a limited-time sale or limited edition, or that supplies were running low, or that it was popular and in high demand?

The focus of this book is the psychology *behind* scarcity and why it has such a powerful impact. When people encounter scarcity, it can be all-consuming—whether for minutes, hours, days, months, or years. From a psychological perspective, scarcity often causes our minds to hyperfocus on the scarce item we might not be able to get. We experience FOMO.

Throughout my 20-year career as a marketing consultant and educator, I have seen scarcity in action and have watched how it influences us to make unplanned purchases or sign contracts even though we may feel uneasy about signing on the dotted line. After earning my PhD in general psychology, successfully completing my own study of scarcity, and continuing my related research, I have discovered some surprising—and sometimes alarming—details about this effective influence factor. Yet this research is mainly in academic journals and not easily accessible to the mainstream public. I felt compelled to make this information available to everyone. It is important to know, from both a business and consumer perspective, why the perception of scarcity leads to purchases and increased sales.

We need to understand scarcity because it is driving our decisions as well as those of our customers. It is a force that can be used to move the needle and trigger action. Whether you are a marketer, salesperson, business owner, online seller, academic researcher, or consumer, scarcity impacts you.

The chapters ahead will look at scarcity from multiple perspectives. There are numerous case studies, research findings, and interviews with current and former executives from various brands including McDonald's, Harry & David, and 1-800-Flowers.com, as well as famous entrepreneur, *Shark Tank* investor, and inventor of the informercial, Kevin Harrington. Additionally, customers' firsthand experiences (with names changed to protect the customers' identities) and anecdotes are woven throughout the book to illustrate and provide an understanding of how scarcity works, when it should be applied, and when it should be avoided. Even as an experienced marketer with a PhD in psychology, I fall for scarcity tactics more often than I care to admit.

Part One of this book, "Understanding Scarcity," covers everything from types of scarcity to the way scarcity messages affect our brains, giving you a deeper understanding of why and how scarcity works. In Part Two, "Using Scarcity," we will get more tactical, and you will discover how scarcity is applied and what makes it effective. The techniques you learn can be applied to your business or personal life. You will also discover when scarcity should be applied and when it should be avoided. Each chapter includes a list of Key Selling Points about scarcity that you can apply to a variety of situations you face.

Scarcity is a tremendous force. Use it correctly.

Let's get started so you can learn now.

# PART ONE

# UNDERSTANDING SCARCITY

# CHAPTER 1

# Scarcity as an Influence Factor

THE DINNER PLATES HAD just been cleared. John was nervous and kept fiddling with the box hidden in his pocket. Was now the time? He had practiced the words all day—would he get them right? He took a deep breath, pushed back his chair, and dropped to one knee. He slowly pulled out the velvet box and quietly pushed open the lid. Nestled inside was a 1.5-carat round diamond set in a slim white gold band. As the other restaurant patrons looked on, John asked the question, "Will you marry me?"

A diamond is forever.

This is a statement that has been embedded in our minds since the 1940s with little question as to its validity. But how could that be? Diamonds aren't forever. They can shatter. They can chip. They can be burned into mere ashes.

Yet we associate diamonds with wealth, status, and above all else . . . romance. We hold on to diamonds and pass them down to the next generation. We believe that diamonds are meant to be kept for as long as we are alive. Some of us even end up getting buried wearing them.

This perception we have of diamonds resulted from a well-crafted strategy designed to increase diamond sales worldwide.

In 1938, a 29-year-old Harry Oppenheimer traveled nearly 8,000 miles with the goal of keeping his family's company profitable.

Oppenheimer, the son of the chairman of De Beers, embarked on this journey that would forever change the way we view diamonds and would solidify De Beers's position as the leader in a multibillion-dollar industry. At that time, De Beers was the world's largest producer and distributor of diamonds, but market conditions were threatening the company's existence.

The price of diamonds had dropped, causing instability and uncertainty in the diamond market. Diamond prices had collapsed in Europe during the Depression, and diamond engagement rings had not been the standard choice in many European countries, including Germany, Italy, and Spain. Other gemstones were still preferred and popular. In the United States, the idea of including a diamond in an engagement ring was gaining traction, but slowly. To make matters worse, those diamonds were smaller and of poorer quality than those sold in Europe. Once a man gave his fiancée an engagement ring, the probability of him purchasing another diamond was next to zero.

De Beers couldn't change the economy, but it could take steps to change perceptions. As Stefan Kanfer, author of *The Last Empire*, so eloquently put it, "Consumers were made, not born."[1]

In other words, it is the *perceived value* of the product or brand that will turn someone into a customer.

For De Beers to be able to control demand, and therefore prices, a significant shift in the perception of diamonds was needed. The public needed to view diamonds not as precious stones that can and should be resold, but as a symbol of lasting love and commitment.

To put it simply, De Beers needed to do something to stop its profits from declining before it was too late.

Oppenheimer's bankers had encouraged him to contact N. W. Ayer, one of the largest US advertising agencies at the time, to develop a campaign that would change consumers' perceptions about diamonds and convince them to buy more of them and in bigger sizes. Oppenheimer's meeting with Gerald Lauck of N. W. Ayer was the catalyst in diamonds becoming synonymous with romance.

Oppenheimer convinced Lauck that N. W. Ayer should create a plan to improve the image of diamonds among consumers in the United States. Assuring Lauck that De Beers had not contacted any other agencies and would underwrite the research involved, N. W. Ayer signed on.

After extensive research, N. W. Ayer concluded that the association between diamonds and romance needed to be strengthened and solidified. At that time, young men purchased over 90 percent of all engagement rings; they were the ones who would need to be convinced that the ultimate expression of everlasting love was a gift of diamonds. The plan developed by the ad agency focused on making diamonds synonymous with romance. While economic conditions could not be influenced, consumers could.

Just two years after the initial meeting between Oppenheimer and Lauck, US diamond sales grew by 55 percent because of the steps taken to persuade consumers.

Fast-forward nine years to 1947, and the ad agency hatched a new plan that relied heavily on psychology. The strategy was to enforce the tradition of the diamond engagement ring and to position it as a psychological necessity. The target audience was the 70 million people ages 15 and over who could be potentially swayed in their view of diamonds. Part of the proposed plan was shocking. It included a series of lectures in high schools around the country that would revolve around the diamond engagement ring. In a confidential memo to De Beers, N. W. Ayer explained that "all of these lectures revolve around the diamond engagement ring, and are reaching thousands of girls in their assemblies, classes, and informal meetings in our leading educational institutions."[2] The lecture program reached thousands of high school girls and instilled in their minds that diamonds and becoming engaged were inextricably linked.

There were other tactics taken during the first several years of the ad campaign to continue to influence consumers and create demand for diamonds.

A year later, in 1948, a copywriter at N.W. Ayer came up with the timeless motto, "A diamond is forever," which some consider the greatest advertising slogan of the twentieth century. Subliminally, the message was to keep the diamonds you received and never resell them. De Beers couldn't risk a surplus of diamonds flooding the market if it were to keep diamond prices steady. The perception of scarcity would also be shattered.

When the movie *Gentlemen Prefer Blondes* was released in 1953, the message, already loud and clear, was amplified when Marilyn Monroe and Jane Russell sang "Diamonds Are a Girl's Best Friend." The demand for diamonds grew.

What does this story have to do with scarcity? Everything.

Limited supply and popular demand are both reasons why scarcity exists. If there is a limited supply of something, meaning there just aren't that many available, scarcity occurs. If there is popular demand that leads to a product running low in stock, scarcity occurs. In this story about De Beers, the company used both of these scarcity approaches. De Beers limited the supply of diamonds through its South Africa–based cartel that gave the company control over all aspects of the diamond trade. By instilling in consumers that "diamonds are forever," De Beers subliminally suggested that diamonds should not be resold. Then, with the help of N. W. Ayer, De Beers also increased the demand for diamonds. This put De Beers in a position where it could control diamond prices through artificial scarcity. When something is scarce, it is viewed as valuable. Diamonds were thought to be scarce, resulting in an increase in their value. Scarcity is, of course, not limited to diamonds, as it reaches across many product lines and industries. It also causes us to do things that we otherwise wouldn't. Take the next story as an example.

## SCARCITY STARTS AT A YOUNG AGE

My friend Trevor is not a morning person, and yet there he stood on a chilly Saturday morning, waiting in line outside a major retail toy chain with his eight-year-old son. With a steaming cup of coffee in hand, Trevor looked around at the people in the crowd, all of whom were bundled up in jackets and blankets. There was a mixture of weary parents, excited kids with huge smiles, and young adults sipping energy drinks.

Trevor wondered why he was willing to get up so early to stand outside in a long line in the cold.

Then he looked down at his own smiling child and remembered. His son wanted the hard-to-find Nintendo Switch. His son had heard that this particular retail location was getting a new shipment that day and begged his father to buy him one. It was 2017, and the consoles sold out within minutes of being restocked. Trevor was skeptical and thought the scarcity of the console was an intentional marketing tactic, but his son had convinced him it was worth waiting in line for the chance to get one.

In reality, the Nintendo Switch shortage was due to popular demand—and in Japan, production could not keep pace with the market's need for the Switch. To compound the shortage, scarcity only made people want the Switch even more. Devoted Nintendo fans spent months trying to get their hands on one. Amazon sellers were charging a premium for the consoles. Walmart, Target, and GameStop all struggled to meet demand both in stores and online.

While diamonds and Nintendo Switches are two completely different products with different target audiences, they do share a common thread: scarcity. One might have been driven by artificial scarcity while the other by popular demand. Either way, what we know about scarcity is that it can influence people, whether it was created intentionally or not.

Even at a young age, scarcity can influence us. One study explored this phenomenon by conducting a scarcity experiment with children.[3] Thirty-two children, all of whom were six years old, were asked to choose between scarce and nonscarce items. Whether the item was scarce wasn't known to the child until the moment he or she had to make a selection. The children were given the option to select from a pile with many items identically wrapped or a separate single item (also wrapped). When offered the choice to select an item between the two, the majority of six-year-olds preferred the single (or scarce) item. Even more interesting, this preference increased if they felt there was competition with their peers. In this case, the participants could choose before the two "competitors" made their choices. These children made sure they received the single (scarce) item by choosing before their competitors had the chance. When the child felt that the scarce item was at high risk of being taken by the other children, there was a greater urgency to select that item.

While this is only one study, it does suggest that a preference for scarce items develops at a young age and is strong when there is the presence of competition. It also suggests that as early as six years old, people may use scarce goods to feel unique or special.

All of us have made purchases at one time or another because we were concerned an item would run out. Maybe there wasn't enough supply, or the item was extremely popular. Whatever the reason, we made those purchases because we felt compelled to. We didn't want to miss out—we may not have even realized that was the reason for our actions. Unknowingly, we wanted an item because either we felt a sense of competition or we wanted to feel special or unique, just like the children in the study.

## THE POWER OF SCARCITY

Scarcity is one of the most powerful elements of influence that affect judgment and preference for an object. There are many factors at play that cause this to happen, but from a broad perspective, scarcity elicits a feeling of threatened freedom to possess something, which increases our desire for that item. People don't want their ability to choose to be taken away. It goes against human nature.

Scarcity, as well as other principles that influence human psychology, can be beneficial in various circumstances, including business negotiations, social interactions, and personal situations, all of which will be discussed in future chapters. Of course, when used correctly and ethically in marketing messages, scarcity can be highly effective. When a scarcity message, such as "nearly sold out!" is added to an advertisement and it is a truthful statement, it can motivate our purchasing decisions. In other words, it encourages us to act, whether that includes making a tangible purchase, donating to a cause, getting a vaccine, or purchasing services.

Throughout human history, we have competed for survival, meaning we have fought to obtain the resources essential for our continued well-being. Our ancestors continuously went through periods of famine and abundance and had to cope with resource scarcity.

According to evolutionary biology and economics, competition always involves scarce resources. The effect that scarcity has now is caused by a combination of deep-rooted instincts and modern challenges. When we encounter scarcity, our nervous systems become activated, and we move into a state of hoarding and greed.

Throughout history, scarcity has also been associated with power. When ancient empires and governments, such as Rome, the Ottoman Empire, and Qing China, were able to secure access to food and water, they maintained authority. They had scarce items that were essential to survival, giving them great control over others.

Even today, people often describe a feeling that resources in their lives are lacking. This feeling of scarcity is often the result of chronic shortages, but this belief also exists among individuals who have relative abundance. The sense of scarcity, or even the fear of its existence, can materialize regardless of one's economic status.

Consequently, many of us worry about scarcity. We tend to prefer scarce items over abundant ones. Scarcity preference can:

1. Be a valued characteristic of the good itself

2. Cause a hyperfocus on what we can't or don't have

3. Simplify the decision-making process

4. Result from a fear of missing out

Scarcity is such an immense topic that researchers have devoted more than 200 years studying its impact. As scarcity research has expanded over time, it has been identified as an influence factor, a cause of psychological and behavioral changes, a catalyst in competition, a way to reduce demand on mental capacity, and a signal of product value. It's even why "playing hard to get" can lead to more dates and more attention—because we desire something more when we perceive it as difficult to obtain, which we will explore more in Chapter 2.

There are many situations that can lead to scarcity naturally, such as a supply shortage due to production delays or capacity constraints (as we saw in the Nintendo Switch example). However, sometimes scarcity is deliberate. Businesses can intentionally create a sense of scarcity by keeping supplies artificially low or projecting the perception of scarcity through promotions or sales (as we saw in the De Beers example).

We react to various cues in the retail marketplace (i.e., product promotions) when making purchase decisions, even if we don't realize that's what we're doing. Savvy marketers have taken advantage of this behavior by continuing to use scarcity appeals in advertisements and promotions. When we become influenced, we act. Most of us hate the idea that our ability to purchase an item might be threatened.

## SCARCITY IS INFLUENTIAL

Persuasion engages innate human responses. When used as an influence tactic, scarcity can change beliefs, attitudes, or behaviors due to actual or perceived pressure. Social psychologists have been especially interested in scarcity and influence because they can cause significant behavior changes and result in people making decisions they otherwise would not have made. As mentioned earlier, items have a greater appeal when their availability is limited or restricted.

We see scarcity often with infomercials, as time is limited to take action. During a conversation I had with Kevin Harrington, an original "shark" on the TV show *Shark Tank*, creator of the infomercial, and pioneer of the As Seen On TV industry, he talked about this concept. He explained, "I was introduced to this whole scarcity way of selling back in the early '80s. Not only was I exposed to it when selling on Home Shopping Network, but also when selling on infomercials. We would sometimes say you must order within a certain period of time to get the product or special offer." With this language, a sense of urgency was created.

Even 40 years after his initial introduction to scarcity selling, Kevin explained that he still sees this concept in action. For example, we talked about big celebrities, such as the Kardashians, and how they use a newer form of scarcity referred to as a "drop." The Kardashians might tell their audience that they will put

10,000 pieces out tonight, but once they're gone, they're gone. Within hours, the products sell out. We see the same thing with a growing number of brands, including Nike, Supreme, Off-White, and even Amazon, which has a program where influencers curate a collection of clothing that is then available for shoppers for 30 hours or less. Guess what Amazon calls this program? The Drop. No matter the phrasing, it sounds very similar to what has been done for decades within informercials and shopping channels.

On the flip side, companies that participate in such drops that tout limited quantities know that over time, they can't continue to drop or promote the same product over and over again. If they did, the effects of scarcity wouldn't exist. That is where limited editions really shine. Home shopping networks have taken a creative approach to this concept.

"QVC might sell the same product for multiple years, and each time it is offered, it sells out. Eventually, we might make it a limited edition by offering a slightly different version of the original product. For example, if it was a 9-piece cookware set, we might make it an 11-piece cookware set by including 2 more lids. It is now a limited-edition product," explained Kevin. The brilliance of this variation in the cookware set is that it is also instantly different from what other stores might be selling.

In advertising, scarcity appeals highlight features associated with the uniqueness, rarity, or unavailability of a product or opportunity. Technology, including social media and other digital sources, has only served to foster this type of influence tactic. As a result, scarcity has become a mainstay approach in marketing and psychology because it tends to improve the effectiveness of advertisements and sales pitches, and it changes behaviors and attitudes.

## SCARCITY AFFECTS THE BRAIN

Not only has scarcity been studied from a psychological perspective; it's also been examined through a neurological lens. With advancements in neuroscience, researchers can now *see* the activity in our brains when faced with scarcity. That is exactly what happened in a 2019 study when participants bid on products in an auction simulation.[4] When the products shown were positioned as scarce, fMRI scans showed that the area of the participants' brains (the orbitofrontal cortex) that is associated with valuation processes had a rise in activity. Participants consequently bid higher on scarce products than nonscarce products. From this study, we know that scarcity can quickly trigger the evaluation of a product's value *and* will result in a swift decision. An earlier neurological study about scarcity also had surprising findings.

In a 2017 study, participants were shown a promotional message that reflected a percentage off the price of a product.[5] There were different variations of this message: some showed the offer was for today only, some showed the offer was for one week only, and some had no expiration at all. While hooked up to an fMRI scanner, participants pressed a button if they wished to purchase the product they were presented with. Each time they chose to buy a product with one of the limited-time offers, the area in their brain that was linked to emotion (the amygdala) had an increase in activity. The same could not be said when the product offering wasn't considered scarce. The researchers also found that when someone made the decision to buy the scarce product, information that did not favor the person's decision to buy was essentially ignored.

What these two studies tell us is that scarcity may increase your sense of urgency to make a decision, leading to a mentality of "buy it now." This thought process hinders our cognitive ability to analytically process costs and benefits in a sensible manner. Instead, our cognitive resources become focused on processing why we *should* buy something, and they suppress any other thoughts that may impede the decision to purchase.

These studies, which are among the many that have measured brain activity related to scarcity, prove that scarcity isn't a made-up influence factor—it's something you can actually see happening in the brain through fMRI scans.

Our brains are hardwired for survival, which is why we often focus on what we don't have. Scarcity causes our brain to shift its focus onto what it considers urgent. If there is something we really want to buy that's also hard to get, our brains shift into gear and place mental energy and focus on rectifying the decision, because from our mind's perspective, this need is now urgent.

For instance, let's consider the McRib.

## LIMITED AVAILABILITY AS THE GREATEST SELLING POINT

The McDonald's McRib sandwich—that boneless pork patty molded into the shape of ribs, slathered with BBQ sauce, and topped with raw onions and pickles—has achieved cult status, mostly because of its scarcity. The McRib is offered only for a limited time; it is not uncommon to see the telltale signal of scarcity in McDonald's ads, "While supplies last."

The iconic sandwich made its debut in the company's US restaurants in 1981 and ran until about 1985. Sales had dropped for the product, which caused its removal from the permanent menu. In the late 1980s, McDonald's decided to release the McRib as a limited-time product and have some fun with it. McDonald's would release it temporarily in local markets around the United States and even in some global locations.

In 2005, McDonald's launched the farewell tour for the McRib, which resulted in tremendous buzz, including a website that was promptly created to save the iconic sandwich. Due to the immense success of the farewell tour, additional farewell tours came out in 2006 and 2007. Then in 2010, the McRib was released yet again, emphasizing the legend of the sandwich. Over the years, chasing the McRib has become a phenomenon and has been the focal point of numerous parodies on TV shows, including *The Simpsons, How I Met Your Mother*, and *Roseanne*. Even on *Full House*, Becky says, "Joey, what's going on? I haven't seen you this excited since they brought back the McRib."

McDonald's has approached the concept of scarcity in a unique way, which is what makes the McRib unique and in demand. The McRib appears only periodically on the McDonald's menu, and the geographic locations in which it appears can vary. This has left people wanting and demanding its release. You never know when and where it will show up, and its limited availability turned into its greatest selling point. Turns out, we like something more when we can't take it for granted.

Over time it seems that the unpredictability of the McRib's release has resulted in a passion for the limited-time McRib and has also prompted bloggers to write about the sandwich, fans to join social media groups to discuss "McRib sightings," and even people to develop websites solely focused on the popular sandwich. One McRib fan, Alan Klein, built the popular McRib Locator website, where fans can locate, report sightings of, and talk about the McRib.[6] Numerous Facebook pages exist dedicated to the sandwich, with thousands of followers. One fan bragged that he had 27 McRib sandwiches over a four-week time span. This fan also explained that during McRib season, he thinks about the tangy pork sandwiches throughout the day. It becomes an obsession for many. They hyperfocus on the limited availability of this sandwich.

McDonald's successfully used the McRib to build brand affinity and long-term loyalty with customers. There continues to be a frenzy among superfans, as they flock to McDonald's restaurants to buy the sandwiches before they go away. It's because of these fans, and ultimately McDonald's brilliance with limited-time offerings, that the McRib has been kept alive for nearly four decades.

## THE MOTIVATIONS BEHIND SCARCITY

Marketers use scarcity to influence consumers by appealing to how they *aspire to be perceived* by other people. If someone wants to be envied or admired by other people, there will be a strong attraction to a product that's exclusive, in limited supply, or a limited edition.

As humans, we have wants, needs, and desires, all of which are at the core of consumer behavior. The idea that something can be here today and gone tomorrow drives most of us crazy, and it's what makes scarcity such a powerful influence in how we make decisions. *Fear* of not having something has existed for time immemorial. While this fear can be associated with essential things such as food, water, and shelter, it is also often tied to non-essential material possessions.

We want what we want when we want it. We don't want that air fryer to be sold out on Amazon or eBay. We don't want our time to get that deal or special item to be limited, even when it is. We don't want other kids to get that new Lego set before our own kids do. When our desires are not met, we feel a sense of *loss*. Scarcity causes anxiety because we have a fear of missing out (FOMO). This anxiety can lead to a perceived loss of personal control—and we don't like not having control. When it comes to scarcity, the only way to regain control is to get our hands on the scarce item. When we do, our feeling of control is restored.

## SCARCITY IS EXTREMELY FRAGILE

As powerful as scarcity is, it is a force that is extremely fragile. Using scarcity in marketing messages is a risk—one that should be carefully considered and mitigated. Scarcity must be validated by the person on the receiving end of your message through signals that prove there is some type of limited availability. Consider the following:

- There is a limited-time sale with deep discounts, but no expiration date.

- A company claims that an item is nearly sold out, but a consumer does a quick search online and finds the opposite to be true.

- A retail store announces that product quantities are low, but the shelves are fully stocked.

- The exclusive membership club is always crowded.

- A fashion brand advertises that a new jacket is available in limited quantities, but everyone seems to have it.

In all these scenarios, trust gets shattered and the product's value plummets. Consumers often share information on review sites, discussion forums, and social media platforms. It doesn't take long for a company's credibility to falter when the company is viewed as being manipulative. When it is obvious that a scarcity claim was made to only improve sales, it can irreparably harm a business's reputation, which is something we will get into in Chapter 5.

## APPLYING SCARCITY

De Beers and N. W. Ayer understood the concept of scarcity and recognized that control of demand and supply was key to keeping diamond prices high. Nintendo, although a consequence of production deficiency, witnessed demand for its Switch consoles skyrocket as consumers became focused on getting their hands on the scarce gaming unit. McDonald's sold more sandwiches when it made its McRib available for a limited time instead of permanently.

———

There is no question that scarcity has a powerful influence over us, more than most of us realize, and it can be effectively applied in many ways and in many styles. It is a power that can be used to manipulate and control, or in a more positive light, it can make us smarter about the decisions we make. Once you are aware of the role that scarcity plays in your own life, you'll be able to make better informed and thought-out decisions. In the next chapter, we will explore how we react to scarcity.

## KEY SELLING POINTS

- When a (truthful) scarcity message is added to an advertisement, it encourages us to act (i.e., make a purchase, donate, etc.).

- Scarcity has become a mainstay approach in marketing and psychology both because it tends to improve the effectiveness of advertisements and sales pitches and because it changes behaviors and attitudes.

- Scarcity may increase your sense of urgency to make a decision, leading to a mentality of "buy it now."

- Once you are aware of the role scarcity plays in your own life, you'll be able to make better informed and thought-out decisions.

# CHAPTER 2

# You Can't Have That!

Scarcity wasn't part of Lectric eBikes' plan, but it was one of the major catalysts in its quick expansion and growth. The company was founded by two young entrepreneurs and lifelong friends, Levi Conlow and Robby Deziel. Brent Conlow, Levi's father and the company's champion from the beginning, believed so much in the duo's ability to produce a high-quality electric bike, that he invested his own money, which meant postponing his retirement. At the time I interviewed Levi, the company was 2½ years old and thriving more than anyone could have ever imagined.

I reached out to Levi while I was working on this book because of a conversation I had with a fellow university professor. I was explaining to my colleague the immense impact that scarcity has on businesses and marketing success. Immediately, she asked me if I knew about Lectric eBikes, which was cofounded by a recent graduate of our university. Animatedly, she explained how she had been on a wait list for an electric bike and how excited she was simply in anticipation of getting on one of these hard-to-get bikes. While her story intrigued me, my conversation with Levi blew me away.

As two fiscally conservative and passionate new business owners, Levi and Robby decided that they would "boot-strap" their new business. They had already identified their target audience, 45–85-year-olds who wanted to splurge on a fun indulgence. To fund their operation, they gave customers the opportunity to preorder their bikes. Customers would pay the full amount in advance. This allowed Levi and Robby to use those funds to produce the finished product and fulfill their orders. What continued to happen was demand outpaced supply. There was always a wait list for their electric bikes, which further spurred a perception of value. Lectric eBikes wasn't spending money on advertising; yet sales came pouring in at a consistent pace. If you are wondering how a new company could get people to preorder a product that they've never seen, you're not alone. That was my question, too.

According to Levi, their initial marketing strategy was influencer outreach. They identified eight influencers who aligned with their target audience and could reach that group. They sent a free electric bike to each of the eight influencers and asked them to provide a review if they liked the bike. Well, let's just say the influencers liked the bikes. In fact, one YouTube influencer significantly drove up the demand.

People started coming to the website in droves to order the electric bikes they had seen other people talk about online. However, it didn't take long for those potential customers to realize there was a wait list. That didn't deter them. And they still weren't deterred when they found out the wait could be as long as 8 to 15 weeks. Levi likened the anticipation among these customers to the feeling you get as a child when you're waiting for Christmas. Excitement grew, and these customers would post on social media about the electric bike they were waiting for and also reach out to others whom they knew already had one. In a way, waiting for this electric bike began to create a sense of community among customers. People became enthralled with Lectric eBikes and were quick to share their excitement with others both offline and online.

Scarcity didn't just manifest from the wait list either. Even when there wasn't a wait list, if potential customers came to the website and saw that one bike model or color was sold out, panic would set in. While electric bikes typically have a three-month consideration period, customers would accelerate the decision-making process and purchase a different bike that wasn't sold out on the website. They feared that they would miss out. Levi also explained that they added a countdown timer to the website to let customers know how much longer they had for certain promotions. This timer increased purchasing by 40 percent.

While scarcity drove sales, the quality product and exceptional customer service turned customers into lifelong fans. For many of these customers, Lectric eBikes was a brand they had never heard of. However, they trusted what others (i.e., other customers) had to say. The trust continued to grow as customers would call Lectric eBikes to inquire about their orders. Customers could always talk to someone at the company, which was usually Levi or Robby, who would reassure them that the wait was going to be worth it. Levi said he would end each call with this statement: "I can't wait for you to get your bike because you're going to love it." Based on the success of Lectric eBikes, it's safe to say that love it, they did.

# HOW WE REACT TO SCARCITY

Most of us have heard tales of people meeting up at bars or nightclubs and going home together only to find themselves in the morning wondering what caused them to be attracted to that person. It is such a common occurrence that researchers have done dozens of studies trying to uncover the reason for this behavior. You might have even heard of the most common explanation, "beer goggles." The more beer you drink, the more attractive people get. There is more going on than the obvious.

Research into what is referred to as the "closing-time effect" has spanned over decades and been carried out through countless studies. Some of the findings are what you would expect: alcohol lowers judgment and suppresses inhibitions. Nothing new or noteworthy there. In fact, one of the original studies into this behavior in 1979 concluded that closing time threatened the freedom to choose someone to be with later, and consequently, those remaining in the bar increased in desirability and attractiveness.[1]

The closing-time effect shows how we *react* to scarcity. In 1966 Jack Brehm, a social psychologist at Duke University, conceived the groundbreaking theory that has since been used to explain behaviors today.[2] Brehm's reactance theory focuses on how people react when their freedom to choose is restricted. There are two assumptions made in this theory. One, it is assumed that we have a set of free behaviors we believe we can enact. These free behaviors are actions we have done before, are currently doing, or could do in the future. Two, it is assumed that when our free behaviors are threatened or taken away, we become motivated to restore our freedom. *Our reaction isn't because we desire freedom; it's because we fear its loss. Therefore, we become motivated to restore what we feel is the freedom to choose.*[3] This reactance happens automatically and requires little mental deliberation. It can be so strong that it causes us to make decisions that have negative consequences, such as spending money we shouldn't or buying something we didn't need or truly want.[4]

If you feel as though your freedom is threatened or has been taken away, you will be motivated to regain control of that freedom. If you're told you can't have something, it often makes you want it more. Think of it like reverse psychology. It's one of the oldest parental tricks. We tell our kids, "Whatever you do, don't eat your broccoli." To our delight, they gobble it up. We see this behavior in teenagers as they push for their independence and freedom. When a group of teen smokers were asked during a *Sixty Minutes* interview if their parents' disapproval of smoking had any influence on them, they responded with an emphatic yes. "It makes us want to smoke," the teens responded.[5] It's not just kids and teens, though. Adults can be motivated by something they cannot have, too.

When the college admissions scandal (aka Operation Varsity Blues) hit the news in 2019, what unfolded in front of our eyes was the power of scarcity and psychological reactance. It's common knowledge that getting into top schools, such as Princeton, Harvard, and Yale, is extremely competitive. Not only are these universities known for quality education, but the acceptance rates are as low as 4 percent.[6] With 96 percent of applicants being denied, these institutions have become that much more desirable, and students, plus their parents, will often go to great lengths to get in. And that is exactly what happened with Operation Varsity Blues, a federal investigation that consisted of 200 FBI agents.

College counselor William "Rick" Singer was accused of using a "side door" to get students into some of the most elite colleges in the United States.[7] He allegedly used fraud and bribery to portray these students as athletes for sports in which they had no experience. Singer admitted to conspiring with parents to fix ACT and SAT scores. In some cases, the students weren't even aware of what was going on and/or the measures taken to get them accepted into the schools. Many of the parents were high-profile individuals, including actresses, designers, and corporate executives. Reportedly, they paid anywhere from $200,000 to $6.5 million to guarantee their children's college admission.[8] Nearly $25 million was supposedly paid in bribes to such schools as USC, Yale, Stanford, and Georgetown.[9] Between 2011 and February 2019, Singer used his nonprofit organization to accept the money as donations and then funneled it to his coconspirators at the various schools.

Singer pleaded guilty to charges of racketeering, defrauding the United States, obstruction of justice, and fraud. Many parents also pleaded guilty to their involvement, while others proclaimed their innocence. Those who were found or pleaded guilty were faced with jail time, fines, and community service.

This entire case is closely tied to what we know about scarcity and reactance theory. The schools involved in the scandal all had low acceptance rates, which made them exclusive and desirable. So despite the families' income and social status, these schools were still not easy to get into and in many cases unavailable because either the children's SAT or ACT scores weren't high enough, their GPAs were too low, or there was some other reason that admission wasn't offered. That is where psychological reactance came in. Remember, if you're told you can't have something, it often makes you want it more. You don't want to be told no. Consequently, you focus on restoring the freedom to choose. That is what these parents did with Singer's help. They took steps to ensure they had the freedom to choose an elite school for their children. Scarcity and then reactance.

With reactance theory, it is assumed that we have a set of free behaviors we believe we can enact. These free behaviors are actions we have done before, are currently doing, or could do in the future. It is also assumed that when our free behaviors are threatened or taken away, we become motivated to restore our freedom. That is what we saw with Operation Varsity Blues, and it is also what we saw when the Hobby Lobby coupon was discontinued.

## THE DISAPPEARANCE OF THE HOBBY LOBBY COUPON

"It's been true for as long as I can remember: You don't shop at Hobby Lobby without the 40% off coupon,"[10] explained a blog posted on TheKrazyCouponLady.com, a popular website run by a multimillion-dollar corporation.[11]

Perhaps that was one of the reasons why in January 2021 Hobby Lobby discontinued its weekly 40 percent off coupon that many customers refused to shop without. For years, customers were conditioned to use the coupon on each shopping trip. If they didn't have the paper coupon handy, it was not a problem. They could quickly pull up the online version while shopping, waiting in line, or even standing at the cash register. So what happened?

According to Hobby Lobby, eliminating the weekly coupon would allow the retailer to give "a better value" on "thousands of items."[12] However, that explanation prompted backlash from the retailer's customers. One shopper challenged Hobby Lobby by arguing, "I'm hoping this means you'll make everything NOT ridiculously overpriced then and just make it fair priced to begin with." Another customer commented, "Why don't you just make it the price you want and be done with it? The coupons just seem like a lot of work for everyone."[13]

The strong pushback from Hobby Lobby customers shows reactance theory in action. Because Hobby Lobby had released weekly coupons for as long as customers could remember, customers assumed they had a free behavior they could enact, which in this case was using the coupon. Customers expected the coupons and the freedom to use them. For instance, they might have used the coupons in the past or planned to in the future. Therefore, the first assumption of reactance theory was met. However, when Hobby Lobby discontinued the coupons, customers' free behaviors (i.e., ability to use the coupons) were taken away. But was the second assumption of reactance theory met? You bet.

Remember, we become motivated to restore our freedom, and that is what shoppers did by vocalizing their discontent as we saw in the various comments made on social media.

Although Hobby Lobby tried to appease customers by explaining they would now be getting everyday low prices, it didn't change the fact that shoppers felt like their freedom to use a coupon had been taken from them. While it is unclear if shoppers' reactance to the discounted coupon resulted in lost revenue for Hobby Lobby, what is clear is that many customers were not happy.

Apparently, as adults we are not much different from our younger counterparts. We don't want to be told no, and when it happens, we react. In terms of relationships and human interactions, playing hard to get has often been associated with the scarcity principle. This can happen in our personal and professional lives. Telling a potential employer you need time to think about a job offer or not being eager to go on that first date can both have the same outcome: your desirability to the other person increases. Researchers Gurit Birnbaum, Kobi Zholtack, and Harry Reis conducted a set of three studies to test whether potential dating partners became more desirable when they were perceived as hard to get.[14] In each of the studies, participants interacted with other participants (or at least that is what they thought . . . the other "participants" were really members of the research team). The actual participants were then asked to rate the degree to which they felt the other person was hard to get, their perception of the other person's value, and their desire for that person. When the potential partner was perceived as less available, his or her value and desirability increased. To put it simply, the research showed that we find someone more attractive and desirable when that person is unavailable to us. Yet there has to be some interest there first.

## VALUE YOURSELF FIRST

Dr. Jeremy Nicholson, who is a doctor of social and personality psychology and founder of Nicholson Psychology LLC, with a focus on influence, persuasion, and dating and also known as "The Attraction Doctor," has done extensive research on dating dynamics. Dr. Nicholson agrees that scarcity can cause others to want you more. He doesn't believe it is in the best interest of singles to purposely play hard to get, though. He teaches people that they need to value themselves first and not sell themselves short. They should focus on their specific uniqueness. Doing so makes scarcity become genuine because your value becomes apparent, meaning more suitors. Additionally, you are not going to waste your time with someone who isn't a good match. So you truly do become unavailable. Genuine scarcity leads to retention in dating and better relationships.

Really, these are the same interpersonal dynamics that exist in romantic, business, and other interactions. The experience of Alexa, one of my students, is another example of this concept in action.

Alexa was offered a highly competitive internship at a prestigious accounting firm. After a series of interviews spanning a time period of 2½ hours, Alexa received a call from one of the firm's principals, Joe, offering her the position. Joe explained the details of the internship, including the hourly rate. As much as Alexa wanted the job, she mustered up the nerve to counter the pay. She mentioned that she had an offer from another competing firm (which was true) at a higher hourly rate. This undoubtedly was not the response Joe expected, especially for the internship position. He reiterated that the rate offered was the firm's standard for the position. Alexa thanked him for the offer and asked if she could have some time to think about it. Joe agreed.

Within a few hours, Joe called back to let Alexa know that the firm had agreed to pay her the rate she requested even though up to then the firm had been paying all interns who worked for the firm the rate she was initially offered. So what happened here?

Alexa had made it clear that she had already been offered a position with a competing firm, which meant that she might be unavailable. Because she didn't immediately jump on the offer from Joe's firm, it only fueled the possibility that the firm could lose the opportunity to eventually hire her. Together, these two factors made her perceived value go up and created a sense of competition to hire Alexa.

She did end up accepting the position with Joe at the higher pay rate. Although Alexa might not have ever met Dr. Nicholson, she had followed the advice he gives others. She valued herself and what she would bring to the accounting firm and did not sell herself short.

It's clear that scarcity does cause a reaction, but that reaction can be strengthened or weakened by priming the message. What does this mean? One study involving TV shows will answer that question.

## DO WE ALWAYS WANT TO STAND OUT?

Exclusivity of a product increases desirability, and we differentiate ourselves from others when we have that exclusive item. However, according to a team of professors, feeling a sense of danger can reduce the effectiveness of scarcity messages.[15] This happens because from an evolutionary perspective, we might not want to stand out from the crowd with a distinct, exclusive product when there is danger.[16] This has a direct application to advertising and when a scarcity appeal might be effective.

Imagine you are watching *Law & Order*, and the episode is about a serial killer targeting a specific city or neighborhood. An advertisement begins after an intense moment in the show that highlights a limited-edition product. Based on research, this advertisement would not be effective. Instead, it would actually backfire. The crime drama has primed you for fear and activated a primal response to the commercial. Instinctively, you're pulling away, not wanting to buy something that will distinguish you from others. Think of it this way: Who wants to stand out from the crowd when a predator is approaching? Instead, you want to blend in as much as possible, which comes from the experiences of our ancestors. They were frequently faced with physical threats and had to learn self-protection, which included the recognition that there's safety in numbers. When in a group, you, as an individual, are less noticeable to the predator.

On the other hand, if that same commercial focused on popularity versus limited editions, it would have a more positive impact because you would feel like you're able to hide in the crowd without fear of the predator seeing you.

Now imagine that you're watching a romantic comedy. As you sit and watch an old episode of *Sex and the City*, the same commercial airs. It's advertising the same product with the same scarcity appeal. In this situation, it would have a positive effect on you because you have been primed to *want* to stand out from the crowd. You don't want to blend in because you want to be the most desirable one. This also comes from our ancestors because they had to figure out how to attract a mate, which included differentiating themselves in a positive way. With that in mind, the commercial that shows the popularity of a product, such as a claim that there have been "over a million sold," will backfire.[17]

The lesson here is that the priming of the customer, such as what he or she is watching on TV, can make the difference in how someone reacts to a scarcity appeal.

Another type of reaction we see with scarcity is the increase of competition. My next story can attest to this competitive consequence.

## SCARCITY BREEDS COMPETITION

One spring, my family flew across the country to spend a week at Disney World. My boys, who were 12 and 15 at the time, were less interested in the types of rides I like, such as It's a Small World, Pirates of the Caribbean, and Haunted Mansion—basically anything slow. They were more interested in thrill rides. Try as I might to get them to sit through the Country Bear Jamboree or The Hall of Presidents, they just weren't interested. Instead, they stood in line with hundreds of other people for the fast rides—Space Mountain, Thunder Mountain, and Seven Dwarfs Mine Train. After three fun but exhausting days at the various parks within Disney World, we found ourselves at Disney's Hollywood Studios.

In my family, I'm the travel coordinator—the person who makes the reservations, buys the tickets, and plans the itinerary.

It's not a role I necessarily want, but regardless, it was thrown my way. The night before our Hollywood Studios outing, with phone in hand, I propped my aching feet up (we had walked a total of 15 miles by this point in the week), sipped my wine, and scrolled through the Hollywood Studios attractions listed on the Disney website. I was looking for some rides we could all do together—ones that had enough thrills for my boys, but were also slow enough that I wouldn't feel like I was going to collapse from dizziness right after getting off the ride.

As I viewed the list of attractions, I came across one that caught my attention, Star Wars: Rise of the Resistance. As we were all avid Star Wars fans, I knew my family would be interested in this particular ride. That's not what caught my eye though. Instead, what made me stop and look closer was a message that stated we could join the virtual queue, which was the only way to get on the ride, and it listed two specific times we could join. One was in the morning before the park opened and the other in midafternoon. I thought that was strange, but put no other thought into it except that I would be sure to join the virtual queue first thing in the morning.

I set my alarm for five minutes before the virtual queue would open the day of our visit. Given that I still had not acclimated from Pacific Time to Eastern Time, it was a struggle when the alarm went off. Blurry eyed and still half asleep, I picked up my phone, opened the Disney app, and waited for the exact moment the virtual queue would open. Within minutes, the virtual queue button appeared, and I clicked it immediately. Much to my surprise and frustration, I received a message that the virtual queue was already filled and I would have to try again in the afternoon.

Now I went from only slightly caring about a Star Wars ride to becoming obsessed with it. When we arrived at the park later that morning, I staked out an area that had good phone reception so I could later try to join the virtual queue again. We went about our morning, going on rides, making memories, and waiting in long lines over and over again. As the hours passed, I made sure to keep a close look at the time. My family and I situated ourselves at a table in the center of the area with good phone reception. As the minutes crept closer to 1 p.m., which was when the second virtual queue would open, I started to notice that my heart was beating a little faster and my palms were getting sweaty. What I was experiencing was a physiological reaction, which aligns with reactance theory. I knew that was ridiculous and tried to shake off my own embarrassment for reacting this way to a ride I have never been on, but I still felt that sense of urgency and obsession. We had to get in the virtual queue. I had to restore my freedom to choose the ride. With the app pulled up and my thumb hovering over where the button would pop up, the clock finally struck 1 p.m. I clicked the button as fast as my thumb could move. A message appeared immediately letting me know that we had been placed in a backup boarding group. The group would be called only if there was capacity for more riders.

Now, at the time, I was so focused on getting in the virtual queue, that I didn't realize I wasn't alone. Within our section of good Wi-Fi and phone reception, cheers erupted from the tables around us from people who had secured their places in the queue. Others booed and put their heads down in disappointment. All of this over a ride that lasts no more than a few minutes.

Throughout the rest of the day, I continued to check the app to see if our backup boarding group would be called. The incessant checking of my phone started to take away from my enjoyment of the park with my family. Finally, about one hour before the park was to close, our boarding group was called. We excitedly rushed to the ride only to find that we had to wait in line for 30 minutes with another group. As we stood there, I started to analyze the entire situation. I asked my son why we wanted to go on this ride so badly and what was the big deal. His response, though a simple statement, was profound. He shrugged his shoulders and said, it's because the ride is so hard to get on. The ride (commodity in this example) became more attractive because only a limited number of people would be able to ride. Scarcity caused me to react and compete with others.

The fact that the Disney ride was difficult to get on caused me to hyperfocus on it throughout the day. Initially, though, my decision to try to get us in the virtual queue was quick. I didn't spend time researching the ride and reading reviews. I didn't compare it with other rides to figure out if it was worth the time. Instead, I reacted quickly. My initial decision was based solely on the fact that the boarding groups were limited (we'll dive into mental shortcuts in the next chapter), and I valued the ride based on that knowledge. Something else happened, though. I was in competition with other people.

## INTENTIONAL RESTRICTIONS

When businesses communicate scarcity, it threatens our freedom, which triggers psychological reactance and causes us to act immediately. This action protects our behavioral freedom in a way and is where the urgency to buy arises. Retailers use the concept of reactance to their advantage. Take this scenario as an example.

You are at the grocery store with your weekly list. As you work your way down the aisle to grab one box of Cheerios, you see a sign above the display of cereal that advertises a significant price cut for that week only. The advertisement clearly states that there is a sales restriction. A limit of three boxes per customer. You only need one box, but you feel compelled to buy more. The next thing you know, you have moved on to the next grocery aisle with not one, not two, but three boxes of Cheerios. What you have experienced is at the heart of reactance theory, and if you truly engaged in this behavior, you would not be alone.

Sales at a large grocery store in the United States were analyzed over an 80-week period.[18] During that time, whenever the store would advertise a sale that included a featured product, such as Angel Soft bathroom tissue, Kraft macaroni and cheese, Mazola corn oil, MJB and Yuban coffees, Sparkle paper towels, or StarKist tuna, more units were sold. Featured products that did not have a quantity limit experienced about a 202 percent increase in sales. Not bad. However, when a quantity limit was added to the featured product (such as "only 3 per customer"), sales went up about 544 percent. Instead of only one pack of paper towels, people were buying up to the maximum limit.

Another study had similar results. This experiment was set up at three grocery stores in Sioux City, Iowa.[19] The product: Campbell's soup. The normal price of the soup was $0.89 a can, but a temporary discount was created. A sign was placed behind each soup display stating, "Campbell's Soup Sale—79¢/can." There were three different limit conditions ("no limit per person," "limit of 4 per person," or "limit of 12 per person"). Over the course of three nights between the hours of 8 p.m. and 9 p.m., the purchase limit restrictions were rotated to see how shoppers would react. A research observer covertly watched how each shopper responded, specifically how many cans of soup the individual took from the display.

Let's pause to put ourselves in the shoes of these shoppers. If you were going to save $0.10 per can, think about how many you would buy if there were no purchase limit. Now imagine there is a 4- or 12-can limit. If you were like the majority of shoppers, you would be most swayed by the 12-can limit. The team of professors discovered that when comparing the no limit with the

4-can limit, there was a 9 percent increase in the number of cans purchased. The 12-can limit had a significantly higher impact, though. When compared with the no limit, the number of cans purchased was 112 percent higher than normal, and when compared with the 4-can limit, it was 94 percent higher.

Between these two studies, we can see that purchase-quantity limits cause us to buy more by inducing a need to react. There is another possible explanation worth exploring, but first, let's get back to closing time at the bar.

As closing time approaches, we start to view other bar patrons as more attractive. We subconsciously recognize that our freedom to choose someone is quickly coming to an end, and we react. The remaining individuals become more attractive and desirable. However, this notion has been challenged.

Three researchers in Sydney, Australia, weren't confident that there even was a closing-time effect, meaning that people weren't even reacting to the diminishing options.[20] Using a mix of couples and singles, the Australian researchers discovered that people in a serious relationship showed a closing-time effect equivalent to the reaction of participants who were single. In other words, those in a relationship didn't have their freedom threatened as closing time approached because they had already chosen someone (their significant other or partner). Yet they still found others more attractive as time went on. The fact that both groups—those single and those in a serious relationship—were affected as the hours ticked on and closing time approached suggests that something else was happening.

One of the explanations is based on the mere perception of scarcity and how it relates to value. As people started to pair up and leave the bar, individuals of the opposite sex became scarcer and therefore more attractive. Remember the Campbell's soup experiment? Adding a purchase limit made the cans more valuable to the shoppers.

---

Additionally, there is another major consequence of scarcity that we have yet to discuss. But first, let's recap what we *do* know: Scarcity causes competition. Scarcity increases an item's perceived value. Scarcity makes us want something more. Scarcity causes us to focus on what we can't have. But did you know that scarcity can also lead to mental shortcuts? That might seem to contradict the concept of hyperfocusing on a scarce item (like I did with the virtual cue in Disney), but in reality, it does not. It is simply another effect of scarcity, and the way in which we respond to a scarce product will depend on the situation.

There is an economic principle, known as commodity theory, that can shed some light on the concept that scarcity increases value. We'll explore this concept in the next chapter.

## KEY SELLING POINTS

- We become motivated to restore what we feel is the freedom to choose because we fear loss.

- Playing hard to get has often been associated with the scarcity principle.

- Genuine scarcity leads to retention in dating and better relationships.

- Priming a customer can make the difference in how the customer reacts to a scarcity appeal.

- Scarcity causes competition, increases an item's perceived value, and makes us want something more.

# CHAPTER 3

# Give Your Brain a Break

WHICH ROUTE WILL YOU take to work today? Which online article will you read first? Do you want cream and sugar with your coffee? How will you respond to that email? By the time you climb into bed at night, you will have made hundreds, if not thousands, of decisions throughout the day. According to researchers at Cornell University, 226.7 decisions we make each day are about food alone.[1] Would you like to make that a meal?

It's not just decisions that we face. Every *second*, our senses transmit approximately 11 million bits of information to our brain.[2] When you couple that with technology advances, it's unbelievable how much information we are faced with on a daily basis. Because of all this, our brains have had to adjust so we can improve our capacity for attention. Think of it this way: How many times have you been working on a project and heard the ding of an incoming email? If you are like most people, you stop to check it, and then decide to respond to not only that email message but a few others. Then you decide to look up something online, and the next thing you know, a full 30 minutes have passed. Even if you have the self-discipline to read only that one email message, on average it takes 64 seconds to recover your train of thought.[3] Multiply that by the number of times you stop to check your emails, and it is no wonder you have a hard time focusing.

With these continual interruptions throughout the day, our brains have become conditioned to want everything *faster*.

Each moment of the day, our focus is pulled in so many different directions that we've developed an underlying anxiety to keep track of all the information our tired brains are trying to process. That constant nagging feeling that your brain is tired is not your imagination either. Because we are bombarded with the constant processing of messages, stimuli, and endless decisions to make, we rarely engage in what is known as deep information processing for each piece of data we come across. How could we when we are exposed to literally thousands of messages daily? Instead, we use rapid mental shortcuts to direct our behavior and attitudes. We look for clues or signals that help us make faster decisions.

And this is true for us as consumers, too. We want, or need, to simplify our decision-making when buying a product or service. So to cope, our brains look for shortcuts. For me in the Disney example with the impossible-to-get-on ride, Rise of the Resistance, I took a mental shortcut in making my initial decision to reserve our spot in line. My mental shortcut was *ride + limited availability = quick decision to reserve*. It seems scarcity can lead to mental shortcuts even for amusement park rides.

Give this mental shortcut concept a try for yourself now. Imagine you were invited to a dinner party at a coworker's house. You were told not to bring anything, but you can't show up empty-handed. You decide to bring a bottle of wine. Now you find yourself at the liquor store faced with a lot of options. Because you're not a wine enthusiast or even a wine drinker, you aren't familiar with the different brands. You have a dilemma to solve: Which wine should you bring to the dinner party? You have narrowed it down to Cabernet Sauvignon, but your problem is not yet solved because you must select the brand. One brand only has two remaining bottles on the shelf at the liquor store. All the other brands are fully stocked. You pick the brand that only has two left because you assume the wine must be good if it is almost sold out. You just took a mental shortcut. Your wine decision has been made with a helpful hint from that underlying psychological force: scarcity.

Let's continue this exercise, but with flowers.

Imagine you are on the hunt for a floral arrangement or other meaningful gift. You're not sure what to buy and are viewing the selections on 1-800-Flowers.com. You see that an item has already sold 100 units and there are 200 units left. Taking it a step further, there is a countdown showing the units available in real time. It's clear that the product is popular, and it's very likely that you'll take a mental shortcut by forgoing additional searches and buying right then and there.

Jim McCann, the founder of 1-800-Flowers.com, said his company has seen sales take off when providing this additional information to customers: If 1-800-Flowers.com has a highly popular item that is getting close to selling out, especially around a critical time such as Valentine's Day, the company makes sure to inform its customers. It also lets customers know which product is most popular and when there is an inventory issue. This results in customers spending less time browsing on the site and taking quicker actions, leading to higher conversion rates and happy customers. Customers are satisfied that they have made an informed decision without having to expend too much mental energy. 1-800-Flowers.com has given them a mental shortcut.

Why do we unknowingly use scarcity as a mental shortcut? Oftentimes, we assume that so many buyers purchasing the scarce item can't be wrong. After all, what is the probability that such a large number of people would purchase a bad product or service? Or in the earlier dating example, if someone is playing hard to get because she has other potential suitors, there must be something about that person that is special. To put it simply, mental shortcuts exist when there is limited supply, high popularity, or other forms of unavailability.

Scarcity reduces the time we take to make decisions or evaluate something's value. Think of it like a breather for your brain. Scarcity allows us to process information when we lack the motivation or ability to employ purposeful and careful thinking.

## THE SCARCITY-EQUALS-VALUE MENTALITY

When we use scarcity in our decision-making, whether consciously or not, we tend to equate scarcity with value. Consequently, we often use the scarcity-equals-value mentality to reach conclusions and opinions about something or someone. If you are on the fence about buying that shirt, and then get an email from the retailer that tells you the item is running out, the value of that shirt has just skyrocketed in your mind. And when brands are well known, the chances of us taking this mental shortcut are even greater. Take Tesla as an example.

In 2016, people camped outside of Tesla locations just for the chance to be put at the top of the wait list for the Tesla Model 3. The Model 3 was the first Tesla designed for a mass audience and came with a manageable price point for many consumers. The exclusivity of owning a Tesla, as well as the limited supply, resulted in people handing over $1,000 deposits without hesitation. Remember, this was for a *wait list*. Those customers knew they wouldn't get behind the wheel that day in their new Tesla and drive off. They knew that if they wanted to get their hands on a Model 3, they had to get on that wait list—they had to make a fast decision.

## IF SOMETHING IS SCARCE, WE VIEW IT AS MORE VALUABLE (OR JUST BETTER)

In the De Beers example from Chapter 1, the restricted supply of diamonds and the increased demand resulting from the advertisements created artificial scarcity. Consequently, the price and value of these precious stones went up. This is a prime example of scarcity enhancing desirability *and* value. We will value something to the degree that it is unavailable to us. We typically conclude that if the item is scarce, it must be valuable. Our mental shortcut is *scarce = value = a quick decision*. We don't put a lot of thought into our decision to buy the scarce product; instead we make a hasty decision to purchase *because* the item appears to be scarce. One particular study illustrates this point.[4]

Participants were presented with $25 gift cards from five different stores. The participants were instructed to select four gift cards for a total of $100, and it was explained that three participants would be randomly chosen to keep their $100 worth of gift cards. The participants were told to rank their preferences for the gift cards. One group was told that only a few gift cards were available from each store, and the other group was told that there were many gift cards available from each store. When the gift cards were perceived as scarce, the participants in that group reported a higher level of physiological arousal, meaning it caused them to react to the news that the gift cards were scarce. As we have seen in countless examples so far, this reaction was to want the scarce gift cards more. The researchers concluded that arousal induced by scarcity influences the choices we make when selecting among multiple items in a product class. This concept is apparent not just with "things" (e.g., diamonds, Nintendo Switch consoles, and toilet paper), though.

I have witnessed my students using the same mentality when choosing courses to take. The scheduling interface they use shows them how many seats are available in each class. When they come across a class with a particular professor who has zero seats left, it makes them want to enroll more. They have told me on many occasions that they will start to check the availability of seats on a daily basis leading up to the semester just in case one seat opens up. When I have asked them why they don't just sign up to take the course with another professor who has many seats available, they reply that the instructor must be good because everyone wants to be in his or her class. They're showing the mental shortcut they took in determining the professor's value.

## SCARCITY AFFECTS HOW MUCH WE'LL SPEND AND HOW HARD WE'LL TRY TO GET IT

Of course, value often translates to dollars and is why scarce products drive premium prices. For example, hard-to-get bourbon, illustrated in the Pappy Van Winkle bourbon story as told below, can drive up value and the amount of money that people are willing to pay.

In 2021, a Netflix documentary titled *Heist* told the elaborate story of a massive theft involving liquid gold, aka bourbon.[5] The wild tale that revolved around Pappy Van Winkle bourbon, also known as Pappy, is explained by the "Bourbon King" himself, Gilbert "Toby" Curtsinger, a former employee of Buffalo Trace Distillery, which produces the famous bourbon. Pappy, which is aged 20 years and bottled at 90.4 proof, was considered a rare Kentucky bourbon with a limited production of only 7,000 cases per year. Each bottle would retail for about $130, but an entire secondary market of the hard-to-get bourbon drove an even higher price of $300 to $400 a bottle.[6] Pappy had been dubbed the ultimate cult brand and, according to Buffalo Trace's website, was rated as the number one bourbon whiskey in the world with an impressive 99 out of 100 rating awarded by the World Spirits Championship. As the popularity of Pappy grew, Buffalo Trace Distillery started to warn customers that its supply was not keeping up with demand.

Curtsinger began to smuggle out the highly sought-after bourbon in the early 2000s and sold it for cash, including to the friends on his softball team. Supposedly, in addition to stealing bottles, Curtsinger would load whiskey barrels into his pickup truck, cover them with a tarp, and haul them off to potential buyers. In 2013, the theft of 65 cases of Pappy hit the news.

Buffalo Trace reported the theft to authorities when it was discovered that the bottles were missing. It was estimated that the cases were worth over $25,000. The theft was dubbed "Pappygate."

After receiving an anonymous tip regarding thefts from the Buffalo Trace and Wild Turkey distilleries, the Franklin County sheriff's office secured a search warrant for Curtsinger's property.[7] They found several missing bourbon barrels, and Curtsinger was later arrested and charged for his role in the bourbon scheme. Curtsinger was sentenced to 15 years in prison but was released after 30 days and placed on probation.[8]

There are many factors involved in the bourbon theft, but one that might not be so obvious: scarcity. The bourbon was viewed as rare, and difficult to obtain. That increased its value not only in the primary market, but also in the secondary market where the bourbon would sell for nearly double its retail price. The harder the liquor was to get, the more people wanted it and were willing to pay. They reacted to the shortage and, with Curtsinger's help, took significant steps to regain their freedom to buy it.

## THE POWER OF SIMPLE INFLUENTIAL MESSAGES

It should come as no surprise that advertisers focus less on detailed logical arguments and more on time-tested and simple influential messages, including scarcity appeals. These advertisements are especially effective when you are not particularly motivated or capable to think deeply about a message.

When a company adds a message that a product is low in inventory or back in stock, it gives us the green light to take that mental shortcut and simply buy that item. We are sensitive to complexity, though, meaning if the promotion or scarcity appeal is not simple, we are not going to buy. Businesses can therefore do well by simplifying the scarcity message and/or promotion to make the decision-making process a whole lot easier. Think back to the Campbell's soup example in Chapter 2. Not only is there a reaction to the purchase limitations, but also the limit on the number you can buy at that price allows you to take a mental shortcut. You are unconsciously cued that the appropriate quantity to purchase is the number to which you were limited. You don't have to expend mental energy or engage in deep information processing. It's almost like you are given permission to make that quick decision.

There are a variety of techniques that businesses use to create legitimate scarcity of products and services. Each of the following tactics is effective at encouraging customers to make quick decisions:

- Produce a limited-edition product.

- Temporarily change the product packaging.

- Only offer products through certain stores or websites.

- Restrict the number of items allowed for purchase during a promotion.

- Have a short-term sale.

- Bundle services.

- Clearly indicate when an item is running low in stock.

- Show customers which products are most popular.

- Limit the amount of time someone can respond to an offer.

When customers are faced with these scenarios, more often than not it causes them to take that mental shortcut and greenlight their decisions.

## IT'S A BIT MORE COMPLICATED

If it were as simple as making something scarce or hard to get in order to make more people mindlessly want to buy, hire, date, etc., this book would be done in one chapter. Maybe even less. But it's not that simple. There are some basic factors that must be present for scarcity to cause action: the "commodity" needs to be some-what useful or desirable, it needs to be transferable (meaning one person can give it to another), and there needs to be the possibility that you can actually possess the commodity yourself. In the bour-bon story, Pappy was highly desirable. With the help of Curtsinger, the bourbon bottles and barrels were transferable, and the buyer had the chance to get his or her hands on the coveted liquor.

Let's look at another example. Say, you know a band is tour-ing in your town. You will feel the effects of scarcity if:

1. The band is one that interests you and even more so if tickets sell out fast (desirable).

2. The venue selling the tickets can transfer the tickets (the commodity) to you (transferable).

3. There is a possibility that you can get online and buy the tickets as soon as they go on sale (possession possible).

In this case, all the basic factors involved in scarcity have been met. However, there are other things that can make a scarce item even more attractive, such as first showing the item's value, placing a restriction on availability, making people wait to attain the item, and having only a few suppliers. If you have to make an extra effort to obtain the item, that item has just become more attractive.

In the example of the tickets, if the upcoming sale is pre-announced by the venue, you're now in a position where you have to wait to get the tickets. If you're told you can only buy up to five tickets, those tickets are now even more attractive, and (going back to our grocery store example) it means there is a strong likelihood that you will buy the maximum amount (price permitting, of course).

While the concert example was hypothetical, it was very real for the Bruno Mars Las Vegas concert in 2021. Within minutes, the six shows scheduled for July in Las Vegas sold out, which meant countless fans were left without a ticket. However, MGM Resorts had an option for these left-out fans—the hotel offered packages that included tickets with a total price tag ranging from $2,499 to $6,529.[9] Even though those packages cost significantly more than the tickets, they did include a lot more. "Considering how fast tickets sold out for Bruno Mars's shows, it's probably a good idea to act fast on these packages," cautioned Andrea Romano, a reporter with *Travel + Leisure*.

Knowing or believing that something is scarce can also increase and keep our attention. Some studies have uncovered the phenomenon that adding a scarcity message to a product's package can cause more people to pay attention to it.[10] Although many of these studies were done in laboratory settings, we see the same concept play out all the time. One of the most prevalent examples today involves online retailers.

Retailers often make a big deal about announcing products that were previously sold out and are now back in stock. It gives the perception that these products are highly sought after. If you visit Jack Threads, a popular online men's store, not only will you see a "New Arrivals" section—you'll also see which products were previously sold out and are now back in stock. This insinuates a product is popular, as well as the potential that it will run out of stock again. A scarcity message was added to the product, and now it becomes even more attractive. Scarcity leads to perceived value to a mental shortcut.

Event organizers use the principle of scarcity to sell tickets. Thinking about attending that conference or concert? As soon as you are notified that there are only 45 tickets left, the value of the event just went up in your mind and might have caused you to make that quick decision to immediately buy your tickets. It gives you a completely different perception than if you knew there were hundreds or thousands of tickets left to be sold. However, merely adding a scarcity appeal (e.g., only 45 tickets left) to an advertisement isn't always enough. A study involving a fast-food restaurant came to that same conclusion.

## The Scarcity Message Better Make Sense

Think about how many times you are asked at a fast-food drive-through or sit-down restaurant, "Would you like to add _____ to your meal?" Depending on your level of hunger and the item being offered, you may or may not have said yes.

Dr. Timothy Brock and Laura Brannon[11] with The Ohio State University wanted to find out if setting a time restriction on a strong versus weak message would cause more people to agree to a request. They set up their experiment at a busy, and noisy, Mexican fast-food drive-through restaurant. The restaurant employees taking customers' orders had no idea what the researchers were trying to uncover, but they went along with the experiment. They were instructed to ask customers if they would consider purchasing cinnamon twists, which were rarely purchased. The restaurant had previously tried to promote the sweet treats by touting them as "a [name of restaurant] special." It didn't help much in terms of sales. Brock and Brannon wanted to take a different approach to see if it spurred interest and increased sales. So the drive-through customers heard one of two messages:

> **High restriction:** "Would you like a cinnamon twist made with our special recipe today only?"
>
> **Low restriction:** "Would you like a cinnamon twist made with our usual recipe for this year?"

Order takers also added one of the following statements based on a script:

**Strong argument:** "The cinnamon twist goes great with Mexican food, you know."

**Weak argument:** "The cinnamon twist is not really Mexican food, you know."

After analyzing the data, Brock and Brannon concluded that when the order taker coupled the statement, "Would you like a cinnamon twist made with our special recipe today only?" with "The cinnamon twist goes great with Mexican food, you know," the number of cinnamon twists sold went up. However, when the same restriction ("today only") was used with the weak argument, the number of cinnamon twists sold went down. What was especially surprising about that combo (high restriction and weak argument) was that the sales were lower than when a low restriction and weak argument were given. What this tells us is that scarcity does work, but if you just slap a scarcity message on an advertisement or other scenario, it's not always enough. In fact, it might backfire. You better have a strong overall message or argument to get the maximum result in showing that scarce item is valuable. As academic research and marketers have shown us, the source of the scarcity message is also important in how effective it will be.

## Consider the Source

As much as scarcity leads to a mental shortcut and increased perception of value, the source of the message is critical.

The 2020 pandemic sparked a lot of unusual behaviors, among them the run on toilet paper we discussed earlier. While there will continue to be theories and opinions about this phenomenon, scarcity was at the heart of it. The media continued to report on the toilet paper crisis, which only made the buying frenzy worse. We trusted the news reports and therefore believed that store shelves were becoming bare.

Just like scarcity can cause us to quickly evaluate the worth of an item, the source of scarcity messages can help us cut some corners in our decision-making, too. When you couple the scarcity message with a credible source, your power of influence skyrockets. Many of us are often persuaded because we like or trust the company or person sharing the scarcity message. After all, experts are to be trusted.

One of the reasons scarcity works is because we believe others are also going to be influenced, so it would be smart of us to take action right away. In other words, if you think other people are going to be influenced by a message, you are going to make sure to get your hands on whatever that product or service is before anyone else. As Jim McCann, the founder of 1-800-Flowers.com, explained to me, he saw this phenomenon in December 2021.

Amid the global pandemic, supply shortages were impacting just about every industry. Leading up to Christmas, the media continued to report on supply issues, dock problems, and other logistical challenges that were contributing to product shortages. The underlying message was clear: because there would be a continual decrease in product availability, you'd better start shopping for gifts early. For the first time in 1-800-Flowers.com's history, the company witnessed customers placing gift orders earlier than ever before. Why was this so unusual? In the past, the company had warned customers that the holidays will be here quicker than they know it and urged them not to wait until the last minute. This warning wasn't a marketing tactic, but instead the inevitable result of limited quantities and fulfillment capacities. Jim used Valentine's Day as an example to illustrate this point. The company would relay to customers that if you want roses, or just about any other kind of flower, place orders early because the floral gifts will run out. And it worked most of the time. However, there were still a large number of customers who would wait until the last minute and then couldn't understand why flowers were sold out or why their gift orders couldn't be fulfilled by the required deadline. December 2021 was different. At that time, it wasn't just 1-800-Flowers.com warning customers about product availability issues; it was the media.

Not only was the media a credible source, but the message about product shortages was not self-serving. For 1-800-Flowers.com, and all its associated brands, it was the first time it had ever experienced such a dramatic shift in the demand curve. The media's coverage on scarcity was the driver in that circumstance.

The source of the message, whether it is an advertisement or verbal explanation, provides information outside of the obvious. We will consider the content of the message, but we will also judge who is delivering that content—otherwise known as the source.

## Source Credibility

For scarcity to work within a marketing message, we have to find the source credible. Whether the source is a business, marketer, salesperson, celebrity, or someone else, we will only believe the scarcity message to the extent that we find that source credible.

Perhaps one of the best definitions of source credibility comes from a group of three marketing professors who defined it as the extent to which a "source is perceived as possessing *expertise* relevant to the communication topic and can be *trusted* to give an objective opinion on the subject."[12] In this definition, expertise refers to the source's knowledge of the subject. Trustworthiness refers to the believability of the source, as well as perceived honesty.

Expertise and trustworthiness are major components of cred-ibility, but there is also another factor: attractiveness. A source is considered attractive to the extent that the source is familiar, lik-able, or similar to us.

In many cases, when an expert communicates a message, we actually turn off our brains, meaning we offload the bur-den of the decision process to the expert. Sound familiar? This is, once again, our mental shortcut. We stop thinking for our-selves and wholeheartedly rely on the expert. This might seem hard to believe, but that was the conclusion of a 2009 neurologi-cal study.[13]

Participants of the study were presented with a series of financial choices. With some choices, advice from a financial expert was provided. With others, no advice was given. When the participants viewed the choices that included expert advice, they stopped considering the options and blindly followed the expert's advice. The expert's advice significantly influenced the partic-ipants' behavior. Now these weren't simple decisions, such as where to eat dinner (although sometimes that isn't simple at all!). These were financial decisions that had a level of risk involved. Yet instead of evaluating the options available, the participants trusted the expert and offloaded the decision-making task.

From a practical perspective, businesses need to consider the source when using scarcity as a way to influence others. Will the source of the message be viewed as knowledgeable about that product or service? For instance, imagine that you were exposed to a persuasive message about the importance of a balanced diet. You were told that the message came from a Nobel Prize–winning biologist. The message would be credible, right? It might even change your mind about your eating habits. Now imagine that instead of the Nobel Prize winner being the source, a cook at the local fast-food chain was the source. Would the message be as persuasive? More than likely, you would be more persuaded by the message when you thought it came from the Nobel Prize–winning biologist.[14]

When a spokesperson or brand releases a message, if that source is viewed as having a high level of expertise that is relevant, the chance of changing the minds of consumers goes up. If we immediately *perceive* the source as an expert, we are more likely to buy the product. The important word here is "perceive." Even perceived expertise can cause sales to go up.

When sources are not viewed as experts, the persuasiveness of the message fizzles out.

Let's say you're in the market for a new business suit. You're at Nordstrom looking at the options and a salesperson approaches. She explains that most of her high-powered clients are buying Suitsupply, and there are only a few left in that brand. Prior to hearing that statement, you may have had little interest in Suitsupply, but because the salesperson connected the brand to what others are buying, you now seriously consider it, especially given that the quantity is low. The Nordstrom salesperson acted as the source, and you subconsciously (or consciously) viewed her as the expert.

One study investigated the concept of "expert power" and found that a mere one exposure to the combination of an expert and an object results in a long-lasting positive attitude toward the object.[15] It even has a positive impact on our memory. The research group came to this conclusion after witnessing the brain activity of participants using fMRI scans. Viewing messages from experts actually disrupted brain activity.

Outside of retail, a salesperson can effectively use scarcity to show his or her expertise. For example, a real estate agent makes the claim that she purposely limits the number of clients she takes but might have an opening available. You might not accept a statement like this at face value. Instead, you will probably research the agent first. You might conduct an online search of her name or view her LinkedIn profile to see if the agent is indeed an "expert." The information you find must bolster the real estate agent's perceived expertise, whether that means she posts informative content on LinkedIn or maintains a blog with helpful and authoritative content.

Experts can also be other customers that fall into a category of "people like me." They are customers that you perceive as similar to you in terms of interests, demographics, or other characteristics. Many online companies couple the "people like me mentality" with scarcity messages.

Net-a-Porter, an online luxury fashion retailer, displays a banner of products other shoppers are buying and putting into their shopping carts. Customers can see what people in other countries are buying in real time, which provides a sense of credibility and trust.

During one of my classes at the university, I asked my college students a simple question, "Have you ever been influenced to buy a product from a brand you didn't know after seeing an ad on Instagram?" This question was one I had asked before and is meant to spur the discussion about the power of social media marketing and brands fighting to get our attention. One student, Stacey, immediately raised her hand. She went on to describe a situation in which she had seen an ad while scrolling through her Instagram feed that featured an image of a women in a "cute dress" with a caption that said "Flash Sale: Everything 20% Off Today Only." Stacey said that she didn't recognize the website but still proceeded to click on the ad and begin to fill her online shopping cart. Even with the 20 percent off, Stacey had managed to add $100 of merchandise in her cart. As a college student, $100 was a significant amount (even a noncollege student would consider this a lot of money). She had already gone through the steps of the purchase process and was about to hit the final button to complete her order when she stopped to think about what she was doing. The impulse to take advantage of the limited-time offer caused her to skip the step she would normally take when she was unfamiliar with a particular website, which is research the company online. She opened another tab on her web browser and started to search for reviews about this company. To her surprise, they were nearly all negative. Consumers complained that the quality of the clothes was shoddy, that they looked nothing like the pictures, and that customer service was very poor. There were even some reviews that complained about the incredibly slow shipping, despite what was promised on the e-commerce site. Despite the great discount, Stacey did not move ahead with her purchase.

---

It's important to note that as much as scarcity (and the message source) can cause us to place a higher value on a scarce item and result in us taking mental shortcuts and not engaging in deep information processing, it can also become an obsession, leading to a fear of missing out.

## KEY SELLING POINTS

- Mental shortcuts exist when there is limited supply, high popularity, or other forms of unavailability.

- Scarcity reduces the time we take to make decisions or evaluate something's value.

- Scarcity enhances desirability *and* perceived value.

- Scarce products drive premium prices.

- Strong overall messages or arguments get the maximum result when showing that a scarce item is valuable.

- For scarcity to work within a marketing message, we have to find the source credible.

# CHAPTER 4

# FOMO: Why We're More Afraid of Loss Than We Are of Gain

MIKE WAS IN A line 10 people deep at the popular local BBQ restaurant. It was a casual dining experience where you order at the counter, grab your number, and seat yourself at an open table. Mike was faced with the midweek lunch crowd, who must also have had the same hankering for smoked meats and creamy sides. It had been several minutes, and Mike inched forward in line. As he reached the sixth spot in line, one of the employees came out from the back kitchen to inform the customers waiting that there were only a few of the specials left. Mike started to get anxious. How many were a few? What if the people in front of him all ordered the special; would he be able to get it? The anxiety rose as Mike approached the cashier to order. "I would like the special, please." Mike took a sigh of relief because he got the last special. He smiled because of his good fortune, took the placard with his order number, filled up his drink at the soda fountain, and then took a seat at a table to wait. It was only then that he looked up at the big menu behind the cash register and thought, "Dang it. I wanted the ribs."

Sometimes the fear of loss overshadows potential gain.

## GREATER FEAR OF LOSS THAN GAIN

Advertising is based on one thing, happiness. And you know what happiness is? Happiness is the smell of a new car. It's freedom from fear. It's a billboard on the side of the road that screams reassurance that whatever you are doing is okay. You are okay.

DON DRAPER, *MAD MEN*

Black Friday is notorious for "aggressive" shopping and crowded stores. We research deals in advance, map out which stores to hit first, and decide what products to snatch up. We don't want to miss out on the temporary price discounts, whether we're buying a television at Target or a laptop at Best Buy, so we wait in long lines outside the store and battle other shoppers to get our hands on the deeply discounted items. But why does that happen? Is it just our desire to get a good deal?

As much as we like to gain "things," whether it's wealth, opportunities, relationships, products, etc., the fear of loss is often a greater motivator in our decisions. We also don't want to regret not taking action. This aversion to loss is one of the main reasons that insurance companies emphasize the cost of an unlikely consequence without insurance—it activates our preference to avoid such loss and to buy the coverage. Take these scenarios as examples:

- We are more sensitive to price increases than price decreases.[1]

- A political candidate earns more votes by warning us that if we elect his opponent, our country will become entangled in international conflict.[2]

- An antismoking commercial focuses on someone dying from throat cancer to warn people away from smoking.[3]

These types of situations cause us to focus on a negative outcome that could occur, and from what psychology tells us, loss aversion affects our emotions. Time and time again people rate the pleasure of gaining something lower than the pain of losing that same "something." For this reason, fear-inducing communication has been found effective in persuading people to do things, such as improving dental hygiene and driving safer. However, there is such a thing as going too far. A fear-arousing message that is too strong can cause people to feel threatened. When that happens, the tendency is to become defensive and ignore the message.[4]

One of the fundamental aspects of human behavior is the ability to identify and process changes in our environment and adapt our decisions accordingly. Think about it in a social context. We are likely to change our behavior depending on if we are getting positive or negative feedback from our peers.

Our aversion to loss impacts our decisions and is part of our physiological makeup. The amygdala region of our brain, which is responsible for fear and threat processing, becomes activated when we perceive potential loss. That is the same part of the brain that caused our ancestors to adapt their behavior and flee from potential threats to survive. Survival depended on avoiding negative situations. Avoiding pain meant a greater chance of survival. It's not just our ancestors, though. When we sense or fear loss, our brain is activated and our behavior is affected. We have an emotional response that influences our decision-making. Of course, missing out on a sale or holding a coupon that expires the next day is different from being chased by a saber-toothed tiger. Our ancestors' potential loss was much more detrimental. Yet neurological studies show us that the same part of our brain becomes engaged, no matter the extent of the danger.[5]

Our preference for scarce products is often driven by our fear of loss—of what we might miss out on if we don't compete for the scarce item. We have a greater fear of what we might lose instead of what we might gain. Take lottery tickets as an example. Suppose you were given a lottery ticket by someone, but before the winning number was drawn, you were asked to trade it for a different ticket. Would you do it? According to numerous studies over the years, the answer is likely no.[6] It is easier to imagine a scenario in which the original ticket wins and the new one does not. The anticipation of this possibility is what keeps you from trading that lottery ticket. Loss hurts.

Even if you were offered an incentive to exchange your ticket, research has shown time and time again that you would still be reluctant to give up your original ticket.[7] That might seem strange, because from a statistical perspective, your odds of winning haven't really changed. The explanation for this somewhat irrational behavior is that *we anticipate regret more than we predict potential gain.* Imagine trading your ticket and then finding out that it was the winning number and you lost out on a financial windfall. You would kick yourself for years to come. In your old age you would still be talking about what could have been, had you not made that one fateful mistake.

During an experiment, Nobel laureate Daniel Kahneman discovered that losing $100 was significantly more unappealing than winning $100. How significant? Winning the money was nearly half as appealing as compared with losing the money was unappealing.[8] One of the greatest American tennis players, Jimmy Connors, summed up loss aversion well. Connors was the number one tennis player in the world for more than five years straight. When he was asked what motivated him to perform at such an exceptional level, he gave a profound answer: "I hate to lose more than I love to win."[9] Can't the same be said from a consumer perspective? We hate to lose out on a deal more than we love to "win" that product.

This loss aversion scenario regarding lottery tickets is not a one-off situation. In school, earning extra credit is a big deal and can motivate students to take the additional actions to get a better grade in class. Two professors from California State University San Marcos, Vassilis Dalakas and Kristin Stewart, created an experiment to test whether framing an incentive as a potential gain versus loss was more effective.[10] The incentive, based on students' answering quiz questions correctly throughout the semester, was the option not to take the end-of-semester exam.

The students in one class were told that if they earned enough quiz points, they could skip the exam. The students in the other class were told that the final exam was optional, but only if they earned enough quiz points in the semester; otherwise they would be required to take the exam. The incentive was the same, just framed differently. Professors Dalakas and Stewart discovered that students were more motivated when the incentive was positioned as a potential loss.

## BUSINESSES USE FEAR OF LOSS TO THEIR ADVANTAGE

The fear of loss also can cause us to compete with other consumers. We start to feel an urgency to get the scarce item before it is gone. A movie ticketing platform realized this fact and was able to nudge customers to purchase.

The company, which allowed you to buy movie tickets in advance of heading to the theater, faced a unique challenge years ago. It had a fear-based product. What was the fear? Movie tickets selling out, but the reality was that very few movies actually sold out.

According to one of the company's principal user experience (UX) designers, the challenge the company faced was that, on average, the customer lifetime value was equal to only 1.2 or 1.5 tickets. The company needed a way to entice moviegoers to continue to buy their tickets in advance. Surprisingly, an accidental purchase of a marketing tool by an employee put the company on a trajectory that would not only overcome this challenge, but also create a model that would be followed for years to come.

The "magic" marketing tool included high-powered technology with heat maps and behavioral tracking. With the help of this technology, the movie ticketing company could now see exactly how customers interacted on the website. With this tool in the company's arsenal, the UX design team decided to test various demand-related scarcity messages to see if customers were sensitive to a "nudge."

The UX design team found that not only were customers sensitive, but depending on the message, it could actually have the opposite effect and cause customers to not purchase tickets. If the message was too strong, people wouldn't buy movie tickets because they were worried the theater would be crowded. The scarcity message only worked when it was soft. But what exactly did that mean? To answer that question, we need to get into more details about the testing that was done.

The designers found that for scarcity to work for them, two questions first had to be answered: Is the message believable? Are there other options (e.g., low switching costs because of other theaters in the area)? The company knew a couple of things to answer these questions: the density of the number of theaters in the area and the size of each theater.

The company would use geolocation data to determine how far people were willing to drive in each area. For instance, people in the metro Denver area would drive upward of 50 miles to a movie theater. Yet customers in New York City wouldn't travel farther than a few miles. The potential box office of the movie had to a be certain size, too. If it was too large, everyone would already know about the seating capacity, and a scarcity message would not have the same impact as it might otherwise have. In addition, there were other factors to take into account, like the day of the week, the time of day, and the movie genre. For example, nobody goes to a horror movie on a Saturday night (fear doesn't exactly scream romance). However, horror movies did have a low switching cost, so they were the ideal test for the movie ticketing company, so the UX design team strategically placed a scarcity message on web pages selling horror movie tickets. After hundreds of tests, it was determined that the best scarcity message was "good tickets selling out fast," which was placed on a small bar with an orange gradient fill.

With this data in mind, the movie ticketing company rolled out this specific scarcity message to more movies at box offices across the nation.

The results that followed were nothing short of amazing.

Weeks later, an executive at the company came running down the hall of headquarters demanding an explanation for why the box office sales for Saturday morning movies had risen significantly. In fact, ticket sales had increased by 33 percent. Revenue per box office window had skyrocketed by $100,000. When you multiply that number by the amount of box office windows throughout the country, the increase was substantial. It was the only time in the company's history this had happened—and it was a result of simply changing the placement of the scarcity message, "good tickets selling out fast," next to the name of the movie theater.

In this example, the success of the scarcity message was based on a few factors. The message had to be believable. The message couldn't be too soft or too hard. And the message had to be placed in such a way that it would catch people's attention. The combination of these factors led to the significant bump in the movie ticketing company's revenue.

## URGENCY IN SALES PROMOTIONS

Similar to supplies running out (whether that's movie tickets or toilet paper), a sense of urgency is what makes sales promotions effective, too.

The very purpose of a sales promotion is to encourage consumers to hasten their purchases or even buy larger quantities. In some cases, sales promotions can also spur consumers to switch brands entirely. For companies to realize these benefits, they typically place an emphasis on the promotions' expiration date. It's therefore not uncommon to see such statements as "2 days only!" or "limited time offer" in their advertisements. Sometimes it is not simply the product itself that people fear they will lose out on. It's the bragging rights. People who pride themselves on being first adopters of technology products will line up in front of Apple stores to ensure they are among the first to get the latest iPhone. In that type of scenario, a promotion isn't always necessary to drive sales. Instead, a business can emphasize the pride of being one of the first among friends to have the latest product.

Exclusive offerings, short-term discounts, and low-inventory announcements are all ways that businesses use fear of loss to their advantage. Coupons work the same way. They create fear of loss because while they initially give a perception of potential gain (saving money), as time goes by, they evoke a feeling of potential loss. We fear that we will lose money if we don't use the coupon.

Empirical evidence shows that the closer the expiration date of a manufacturer's coupon, the higher the redemption rate.[11] When we first receive the coupon, we frame it in our minds as a potential gain: "Think of all the money we will be able to save by using this coupon!" Manufacturer coupons, unlike in-store coupons, tend to have a window of anywhere from two to three months from the time the coupon is distributed to when it expires. As time ticks away, we reframe the way we think about the coupon. No longer do we think of the potential gain. We have now reframed our thinking about the coupon as a potential loss. And we're not alone. Other people are feeling the same thing, and consequently, there is a sharp increase in the redemption of the coupon.

This fear of loss can also be used to explain why temporary discounts tend to perform better than everyday low prices. These common offerings don't have a time component, meaning they're offered on a regular basis. If you see the price for $5.00 one week, you won't fear that it will go up to $5.50 the next. On the other hand, a coupon or limited-time price cut signals that the promotion *is* going to end soon end and won't be offered again for a while.

All of this points to why businesses can, and often do, use this strategy of relying on the fear of loss to accelerate purchases.

## TO BUY OR NOT TO BUY

FOMO (fear of missing out) is deep within our subconscious and drives our decisions. FOMO has been explained as a combination of a mental state and emotional change that leads to actions, including consumption.

Melinda Maria Jewelry, a popular yet affordable jewelry brand that is often worn by celebrities, is a great example of how FOMO can increase customer interest and ultimately sales. While the brand has a wholesale division, approximately 95 percent of sales are direct to consumer.

Before realizing the attraction to sold-out products, Melinda Maria Jewelry approached inventory with the mindset that the company needed to go deep into each style to ensure there was enough quantity to meet demand. Yet during the company's period of hypergrowth, the popular jewelry brand realized that selling out of products was not a bad thing.

When I spoke with Melinda Spigel, the founder of Melinda Maria Jewelry, she explained that a sold-out or restocked product affected sales. And in a good way. Going back to the concept of loss aversion, customers don't want to miss out on the opportunity to purchase a product. And that is what continues to happen among customers of Melinda Maria Jewelry. Restocks, preorders, sellouts, and wait lists have only driven customer demand and consequently sales. As Melinda explained, while the staff are waiting for one inventory order to be fulfilled, they are already ordering more to keep up with the demand of preorders.

Along the same line, Melinda Maria Jewelry has also discovered through A/B testing that emails with the word "restock" in the subject line have a substantially higher open rate compared with versions without it. The company now sends "restock" emails once a month, which means it might take the product off the website, readjust the quantity available, and repost it. "Restock" isn't the only thing the company has tested, though.

The brand utilizes data heavily in marketing efforts, which has led to the discovery that when communicating the popularity of a product to customers, sales of that product go up. For instance, sending out an email that says something to the effect of "most wait-listed product" will cause that product to quickly sell out again. Through experimentation, Melinda Maria Jewelry has also found that showing a product with thousands of positive reviews along with the statement to purchase before it sells out again is a catalyst in driving up sales. This aligns with what you learned about in Chapter 3 regarding the "people like me" concept.

"Selling out of products affects how we buy and can lead to a quicker gain in sales. It creates demand and strengthens our brand," explained Melinda.

As of 2020, Melinda Maria Jewelry's wholesale division and direct-to-consumer website reached $20 million in sales.

Of course, there are many factors that can be attributed to Melinda Maria Jewelry's success, including the charisma and creativity of the company's founder, the high quality of products, and the excellent customer service. Yet we still can't ignore the appeal of sold-out goods. Research has shown that we have a greater regret for *inaction*, such as missing out on a chance to buy a style offered by Melinda Maria Jewelry, than a regret for *impulse buying*.

A study involving cruise travelers further explains this feeling of regret.[12]

A group of tourists on a South African cruise were asked to take part in a study while they were traveling and after they returned. They were each given a diary at the beginning of the cruise and told that the researchers were studying satisfaction with items purchased on vacation. What they were really studying was regret. Each day, the tourists were to write down all the items they purchased or thought about purchasing but didn't. These items had to be things they would keep versus give as gifts. They were also instructed to rate their satisfaction, happiness, and regret with each item using seven-point scales.

Three months after the cruise, the participants were sent a follow-up survey about the items they purchased. They were asked to rate each item using the same systems as before. Comparing the results from the two surveys, the researchers discovered that in the short term, participants regretted not purchasing more than purchasing. However, when the second survey was sent out three months after they made the decision not to purchase, they didn't have the same level of regret. The research team followed up their research with two additional studies that came to similar conclusions: right after a limited-purchase opportunity, those who chose not to buy experienced greater regret than those who did buy. In the long term, though, that regret diminished. What the findings suggest is that when we are faced with a situation where the purchase opportunity is very limited, the chance of us immediately regretting *not* making the purchase right away is high. Over time, though, we won't care as much. The concept of immediate regret could be one explanation for the thriving business of many resellers.

## A LIMITED OPPORTUNITY TO BUY

With over 20 million visitors each year, the Magic Kingdom at Walt Disney World in Florida is bound to sell its share of souvenirs.[13] However, with everything to do and all the time you spend walking and waiting in lines, it can be easy to lose the time and energy to pick up a souvenir. Perhaps you even find yourself on the fence about buying a certain item to take home. For this example, let's pretend you didn't buy the souvenir but you realize you should have, so you go on a hunt to find it online. Lo and behold, you find the mug on eBay—but it costs 90 percent more than it did in the park. You buy it anyway, because no one wants to continue to feel regret.

I share this story because savvy online resellers know that there's a market for this exact type of person: vacationers who returned home without that coveted souvenir. Some have built their businesses on this potential regret by going to the theme parks themselves and purchasing souvenirs in mass with the plan to sell them at a marked-up price.

The same concept applies when attending a concert. If you were told the band's merchandise for sale was only offered at that concert, there is a greater chance that you will regret your decision if you decide against making the purchase.

Many marketers and entrepreneurs know that scarcity focused on loss can have a powerful effect on us. If the time window to make the purchase is limited and you do not take action, you might blame yourself and think of what could have been. Based on the concept of loss aversion, a business might consider a promotion where customers get $50 applied to a future purchase instead of an immediate $50 discount. The incentive for the future purchase will be greater. This is a practice many retailers have adopted, including Kohl's, Tilly's, Hot Topic, and IKEA, to name a few.

## A LIMITED TIME TO BUY

Businesses that are effective at capitalizing on fear of loss understand that it all comes down to correctly framing the purchase scenario. You can see this in Black Friday ads. Target might show the discounted prices that are in effect between 6 a.m. and 11 a.m. and compare them with the regular prices. This creates a signal to buyers that if they don't shop during the sale, they will miss out.

Watching items run low in real time is another prompt that leads to possible fear of loss and regret. Amazon uses this tactic all the time. Let's say you're shopping on Amazon for a soap dispenser. You'll likely be presented with hundreds, if not thousands, of options to choose from. Which one catches your eye? It's the one that has a statement in red print at the bottom of the listing, "only six left in stock—order soon." It is sending you the message that if you don't act quickly, you might lose your chance to buy.

Other online sites also use this technique. Ever been on Booking.com? If you search for a San Diego hotel on the site, several of the hotel listings will include the number of rooms left—so you better book soon.

In a subtle (or maybe not-so-subtle) way, Amazon and Booking are saying that if you don't buy (or book) now, you could miss out. The "best" choices will be gone.

## FIND A TREASURE MENTALITY

If you've ever stepped foot inside a TJ Maxx, you unknowingly experienced FOMO in action. This discount retailer purposely makes sure it always has an inconsistent assortment of products. The goal is to create a "find a treasure" mentality. You have to hunt through the store and buy what you can when you can, because it might not be there tomorrow. Just as much as you can find a treasure, you can also miss out on one. This leads to shoppers engaging in in-store hoarding and in-store hiding.

## HOARDING AND HIDING

Not sure what I mean by in-store hoarding and hiding? Let's look at some retailers within the fast fashion industry to understand this better. These companies purposely limit product availability with a short renewal cycle and a limited supply of clothing. ZARA and H&M have both been known to use this strategy.[14]

Most fast fashion retailers plan in such a way that their stocked products sell out within two weeks. Once the inventory is sold, no more is available. Period. This creates the mentality among shoppers that if they do not purchase the clothing item now, it won't be there when they come back—even if that means going to a different section and coming back only minutes later. Because of this, shoppers keep items with them while they peruse the rest of the store's inventory even if they don't know if they want the items: aka in-store hoarding. Hoarding has been recognized both as a way to cope with a perceived risk of a product shortage and as a way to reduce fear.

In-store hiding also results when there is a fear of loss or a perceived risk of an item not being available. Shoppers who hide an item intentionally hide it from other shoppers within the store so they can purchase the item if they decide to return. Doing this increases the odds of being able to purchase the desired item and is a strategy used to overcome the fear of loss and possible regret for missing out on the purchase.

———

As we have learned, FOMO is a big deal when it comes to scarce items because we have a greater fear of loss than of potential gain. Even though this fear might be only temporary, it can impact our decisions, including our purchases. Businesses can capitalize on scarcity and FOMO, but when the attempt is overt or viewed as a sales tactic, it might fall flat. We explore this concept in the next chapter.

## KEY SELLING POINTS

- We have a greater fear of what we might lose instead of what we might gain.

- Temporary discounts tend to perform better than everyday low prices.

- There is a greater regret for inaction than a regret for impulse buying.

- The chance of us immediately regretting not making the purchase right away is high.

- Businesses that are effective at capitalizing on fear of loss understand that it all comes down to correctly framing the purchase scenario.

- Watching items run low in real time is another prompt that leads to possible fear of loss and regret.

# CHAPTER 5

# When Scarcity Doesn't Work

"Spa client irate after being manipulated into bum deal" read the headline in a 2020 consumer watch article published by *Pretoria News* in South Africa.[1] A 32-year-old woman, referred to as "Rania" (not her real name), had shared her story with Consumer Watchdog regarding her experience with a local medical spa.

Rania had scoliosis, which is defined as a sideways curvature of the spine. She was self-conscious about her condition and had opted for cosmetic surgery, but was unhappy with the indent it left on her body. Rania decided to explore the option of fillers and came across a doctor at a medical spa nearby. The doctor had positive reviews both on the medical spa website and on social media sites. Rania had a virtual consultation with the doctor, which according to Rania, didn't include an examination or even specific questions, such as her weight or measurements. The doctor allegedly advised Rania that she would need eighteen 10-cc vials of filler. According to Rania, the doctor further said that she did these types of procedures all the time and that the only risk was bruising. When Rania questioned the risks, the doctor supposedly assured Rania it was completely safe. As Rania recalls, the doctor also went on to say that because the medical spa is so popular, Rania would need to pay immediately to secure her appointment in time for the December holidays.

Rania explained that she felt pressured to take advantage of the deal, so she paid for the fillers that day. After payment, her appointment was not confirmed, and she quickly realized she had been rushed into the deal.

Rania then turned to Google to research the possible risks of the fillers she purchased and came across terrible stories of infections and other complications. She also learned that she was at a higher risk of a reaction due to an autoimmune disease. Because of all this, Rania tried to cancel the appointment but was told there were no refunds. Eventually, she was told that the money could be refunded when another patient had purchased the fillers.

When the medical spa was contacted for the *Pretoria News* article, the doctor responded that Rania was not rushed into a decision and had been told it was risky.

Whether that was the case or not, or if the reality of the conversation was somewhere in the middle, Rania felt a sense of urgency to make her purchase. She perceived that there was high demand because the spa was popular and she might miss out on making her appointment in time for the holidays. Scarcity was the underlying power at work. If we perceive a scarcity appeal, whether in an advertisement or in a conversation, as a sales tactic, it can negatively impact how we view the product or company.

As we have already learned in the previous chapters, scarcity is a significant influence factor that impacts our decisions. Businesses and marketers often purposely limit the supply of a product or the time in which the product is available to create a sense of urgency and increase sales.

In this chapter, we examine when scarcity *doesn't* work, highlighting the scenarios of scarcity being used incorrectly.

## WHAT'S WRONG WITH ARTIFICIAL SCARCITY?

To get started, let's look deeper into artificial scarcity.

Artificial scarcity occurs when the quantity of an item is intentionally restricted, even though there could be enough of that item to meet demand. It can also mean that there is an implied limitation. If scarcity is used, it needs to be used truthfully, meaning scarcity should really exist. It is OK to highlight the scarcity of a product, service, etc., as long as the information is honest and helpful. That leads to a tricky question: What happens when a company and/or salesperson creates artificial scarcity? Perhaps we can answer this question by looking at Ty Inc.'s Beanie Babies in the 1990s and also at some other companies.

Beanie Babies are polyvinyl bean–filled animals created by the US manufacturer Ty Inc., and in the 1990s they were all the craze. The stuffed animals were collected not only as toys but also as a financial investment. One store reported a reserve list for Beanie Babies that was over 10,000, while McDonald's ran a Teenie Beanie Baby promotion that was supposed to last five weeks, but instead ran out of its 81 million "babies" in one week.[2] The mania surrounding Beanie Babies even prompted a book that includes an in-person interview with a man who killed a coworker over one of these stuffed toys and another interview with someone who lives with his 40,000-piece collection of Ty merchandise.[3]

Beanie Babies is a classic example of artificial scarcity. Ty Inc. maintained interest in Beanie Babies by regularly retiring old characters and replacing them with new ones. This opened up a resale market for Beanie Babies where retired characters were sold at a premium in online marketplaces. At one time, 10 percent of all sales on eBay comprised Beanie Babies that had an average selling price of $30, which was six times the retail value.[4] Even more eye-opening is that some of the rarer Beanie Babies got up to six figures.

The speculation was that the Beanie Babies craze would run its course, but in the fall of 1999, nearly six years after Beanie Babies were first introduced, Ty Inc. added an announcement to its website that read, "On December 31, 1999, 11:59 PM CT, all Beanies will be retired"—which was also at a time when the Beanie Babies fever was starting to subside.[5] After making that announcement, Ty stayed tight-lipped, and the buzz surrounding the mysterious announcement skyrocketed. The announcement reignited in-store sales and increased bid volume on collection websites. One store reported a long line of customers waiting outside for the store to open and reported selling nearly 1,000 Beanie Babies in just one day.[6]

Artificial scarcity may have worked for Ty's Beanie Babies, but that doesn't mean it will work for every company.

For example, fashion retailer H&M was accused of destroying new unsold clothing to avoid having a surplus and ultimately to maintain prices. In fact, a student at the City University of New York found bags of unworn but destroyed clothing that had been thrown away by the H&M store in Manhattan. An H&M spokeswoman said that was not the normal practice for the retailer and that the items should have been donated to charity instead. By that time, the story had been picked up by the media, including the *New York Times*.[7] It hurt customers' trust in H&M—and is an example of artificial scarcity working against the company.

## IT'S PRETTY OBVIOUS

Within consumer psychology circles, there is a concept that is often brought up when talking about businesses' and marketers' efforts to persuade, which is referred to as the persuasion knowledge model (PKM). This concept addresses how we respond to persuasion attempts. A study by a German group of researchers shows the PKM in action.[8]

The researchers created an advertisement that featured an enticing image of a fictitious chocolate bar, called "Goodnut," surrounded by cocoa beans and hazelnuts. There were four captions in the one ad:

> "Do something good for the cocoa farmers!"
>
> "Do something good for yourself."
>
> "Chocolate taste."
>
> "Extra high share of nuts."

A Fairtrade logo was added in the bottom corner of the ad as well.

The ad was shown to two groups, and participants were given a survey to complete. In the test group, in addition to seeing the ad, participants also were presented with this note: "Tactic: By using the Fair-Trade label on the chocolate bar, the chocolate bar marketer intends to increase the sales figures of the product and, therefore, his revenue. The primary goal of using the Fair-Trade label is not the support of cocoa farmers."

Based on the survey responses from over 400 participants, the researchers concluded that the use of unfair and inappropriate persuasion tactics can cause consumers to have a less favorable opinion of products, brands, and advertisers. The study also concluded that on the flip side, advertisers can maximize their revenue when persuasion tactics are perceived as appropriate, fair, and effective by consumers.

So as a business or marketer, how do you know if the marketing message is viewed as appropriate, fair, and effective? By ensuring your message is accurate and realistic and aligns with consumers' beliefs.

Our ability to recognize and understand a persuasive intent begins by the age of eight and continues to develop over time. When we were in kindergarten or first grade, we might have wholeheartedly believed the commercial we saw about the latest toy and its high demand, including the implication that it was better than the other toys out there. We might have run straight to our parents demanding that we go to the store now to purchase it. Yet by the time we turned eight years old, we started to get a bit more skeptical about the advertisements we saw. By the time we reached middle school, we had a certain amount of distrust when it came to advertising claims and sales tactics. We started to recognize persuasive intent and continued to develop our understanding and knowledge.[9]

## WHAT WE KNOW ABOUT PERSUASION

According to the PKM, over time we as consumers develop knowledge about persuasion and use this knowledge to "handle" persuasion attempts. This persuasion knowledge is crucial in determining how we respond to marketing efforts and can be used in a variety of ways to help us in situations where another person or a business is trying to persuade us to do something. It guides our attention in persuasive encounters and allows us to make inferences and predictions. From a broader perspective, persuasion knowledge is what helps us quickly identify a manipulative intent and determine our response.

Let's suppose you are shopping for formal attire to wear to a charity gala. You are at the department store and try on the first garment. The salesperson tells you it looks great on you. What do you think of that salesperson's opinion? Is it self-serving or genuine? Next, imagine that you're shopping on a website and the default product recommendations are the most expensive products. Would you choose the default recommendation or shop around for alternatives?

Your answer to these questions depends on whether you used your persuasion knowledge and to what extent.[10] You might infer an ulterior motive in the salesperson's compliment or the default product recommendation on the website. If you view these tactics as inappropriate or manipulative, you're more likely to discount the salesperson's compliment and avoid choosing the default product recommendation. And most of the studies on persuasion knowledge have concluded that persuasion knowledge and skepticism go hand in hand, meaning this combination often leads to an unfavorable evaluation of the salesperson or business.

───────

Let's look at another example of persuasion knowledge in action to understand this better.

A client of mine, Nathan, had been running his consulting company for three years and had been fortunate enough to grow from having a handful of clients to near 15. His firm was small, with only two employees, and for the first three years of business, he was able to handle his business finances on his own. However, as time went on, the burden of keeping the books was taking him away from running and growing his business. He decided to contact an accountant to take on this workload.

A few months prior to this decision, Nathan had connected with Greg on LinkedIn. He didn't know Greg personally, but they shared many mutual connections, which made him feel comfortable enough to accept Greg's connection request. When Nathan started on the search for an accountant, not only did he ask his business acquaintances who they knew that might be able to help him, but he also searched through his connections on LinkedIn, which led him to Greg. Nathan spent some time looking through Greg's profile and researching him online. What he found satisfied his internal question of whether Greg had the right experience, so Nathan decided to contact Greg.

Nathan reached out via LinkedIn and briefly explained what he was looking for. They scheduled a time to meet via Zoom that same week. Nathan came to the video call with his list of questions ready and was hoping Greg would be a good fit as his accountant. The call started out great. Nathan explained his business and described in greater detail what he was looking for, and Greg went over how he could help. Everything was going very well . . . at first.

Toward the end of the meeting, Greg went over his pricing. He quoted a number for his monthly retainer, but then stated that if Nathan committed and signed a contract that day, he would get a special deal of 25 percent off. However, if he didn't commit that day, the price would remain at the original price he quoted. This completely caught Nathan by surprise because he was not prepared to make a decision right away. He politely told Greg that he needed more time and couldn't commit. Greg responded that he would extend his offer 24 hours.

When they ended the call, Nathan started to get a bad view of Greg. Why would Greg pressure him when he made it clear he needed more time? The next day he emailed Greg and declined. Greg replied with another offer with yet another time period on it. Nathan still didn't accept. By that time, he already had a bad view of Greg and didn't appreciate the high-pressure sales tactic to hire Greg as his accountant.

Within the concept of PKM, when we recognize that someone is attempting to persuade us, we consider the appropriateness of that person's tactics. In the situation with Greg and Nathan, Nathan had concluded, whether consciously or subconsciously, that it was inappropriate of Greg to use that sales tactic as his potential accountant. Nathan relied on topic knowledge (e.g., his past experience of working with accountants).

We form beliefs about the traits, goals, and expertise of the agent (e.g., business, salesperson, marketer, or other communicator of the persuasive message).[11] These beliefs include our general perception of marketers, brands, and salespeople. For example, we might stereotype salespeople as behaving or acting a certain way. We might even have stereotypes of brands—such as believing that more prominent brands have better products. We might form a belief about a specific person, too. For instance, you might purchase your appliances from the same store and from the same salesperson every time because you know what to expect. Your previous work together informed your opinion about that salesperson's credibility, dependability, and product knowledge. All of this contributes to your persuasion knowledge.

Let's stay with the scenario of purchasing products from the same appliance salesperson and store. If you were in the market for a new washing machine, you would likely already have an existing attitude about the various brands available based on trust. You might also be aware of the different features available with washing machines. It's sufficient to say that you would probably walk into the appliance store with topic knowledge (brands you trust and features you desire), and you would draw on this knowledge as you shop for that new washing machine.

## PERSUASION IS NOT ALWAYS VIEWED AS BAD

While persuasion knowledge is used in most situations, that doesn't mean you're actually thinking, "Oh, I will use my persuasion knowledge!" when you are persuaded in some way or another. It just happens. But from a business perspective, simply understanding that these factors may play a part in how people might feel when they are being persuaded can go a long way. How? In a few different ways, actually.

First, persuasion knowledge can help companies avoid blatant and possibly inappropriate sales tactics that will turn off customers. Second, this knowledge can help determine if extra time is needed to build trust (i.e., to overcome the perception of salespeople or a brand). Third, by understanding persuasion knowledge, you will be aware of the fact that things like flattery, rhetorical questions, obvious product placement in television shows, biased sources, expensive default options, and negative ad comparisons can all trigger persuasion knowledge and cause suspicion.[12] In each of these cases, if persuasion knowledge isn't in fact acknowledged, it could make the person purchasing the product or service less likely to buy and might even result in that person taking steps to "punish" the agent as a result, with actions like posting negatively on social media or leaving bad reviews.

All of that being said, it doesn't mean that we always view persuasion attempts as negative. As noted earlier, there are in fact instances when we view persuasion as beneficial. We might still question a salesperson's or marketer's sincerity, but we will also take into account the person's competence or helpfulness. If expert information was provided during the interaction and we felt that the source was credible and knowledgeable, we might still be persuaded to make that purchase or hire the service even if we are aware that we're being sold to.

It's important to remember that even if a message is recognized as a persuasive attempt, the outcome can be beneficial to both the customer and business if the company has taken steps to build trust. One way this can be done is by ensuring that marketing and sales activities are a satisfying exchange for both parties, meaning the customer gets what he or she wants and feels treated fairly, while the business gets the sale at a reasonable price. Another way a persuasive attempt is likely to be more effective is for a business to focus on building long-term relationships with customers, improve customer experiences, and deliver on its promises.

## BLATANT SALES TACTICS VERSUS GENUINE SCARCITY

With August only a few days away in Dallas, the temperature had already reached 90 degrees by 11 a.m. That didn't deter my colleague Paul from keeping his promise to take his teenage son, Mark, shopping for cars. Mark was only 15 years old, and his birthday was still six months away. Paul and his wife had agreed that they would help Mark buy a car once he turned 16, as long as Mark had saved $1,000 of his own money to put toward the purchase. As Paul and Mark pulled into the dealership and got out of the car, the heat hit them immediately. They both started to sweat right away but continued on with their purpose to look at cars.

As they walked around the lot, it struck Paul how sparse the inventory seemed. The lot was only half full, and there were more preowned vehicles than new ones. As they stopped to look at one of the cars, a salesperson, Jack, approached. Right away, Paul informed Jack that they were still six months away from buying a car and didn't want to waste Jack's time. They were just there to look and determine what model they would later buy. Jack shrugged and said he didn't mind; he already sold two cars that morning and had met his quota. He explained that he would be more than happy to answer their questions. And that he did. After answering quite a few questions about the specific vehicle, Paul finally asked the big questions on his mind. Why was the inventory so low? Where were all the new cars?

Jack explained that there had been a fire in a chip supplier's factory in Japan, which had halted production for auto manufacturers worldwide. The story of the fire had even been reported by various news sources, from the BBC to the *Wall Street Journal* to CNBC. The fire occurred during a time when a chip shortage was already threatening the production of automobiles and happened at a chip factory that was responsible for about 30 percent of the global market for the microcontroller units used in automobiles.[13] The fire in this factory only exacerbated the problem. The chip company predicted it would take at least 100 days for production to get back to normal. In the meantime, orders would go unfulfilled.

With the truth out in the air that the available supply of vehicles was extremely low, Paul anticipated what would come next:

a subtle push by Jack that if they wanted a vehicle, they should buy now because of the shortage. He just knew that sense of urgency was going to be Jack's angle to close the deal that day. But that's not what happened. Instead, Jack candidly advised that since Paul and Mark were not in a hurry to buy a vehicle, they should be fine to wait. The auto manufacturer's plants were just recently back up and running, and there would again be enough inventory available for customers.

Paul was struck by Jack's candor and felt like this was someone he could trust. He took Jack's business card and thanked him for his time. Six months later, Paul and Mark scheduled an appointment with Jack to look at cars once again, and just as Jack had predicted, the inventory was back up. They chose a vehicle they wanted, and Jack ultimately got the deal—along with the commission, of course.

Imagine if the story had taken a slightly different turn and Jack pressured Paul and Mark to "buy now." If that happened and Jack had withheld the information about the plant reopening, he would have risked breaking trust. Paul and Mark would have questioned Jack's motives and viewed Jack's statements as a persuasion tactic. Would Jack have gotten the sale? Maybe, but it would have depended on how Paul and Mark interpreted their interaction with Jack.

When scarcity is viewed as a sales tactic, it can backfire. Consumers want to feel as though they can trust the salesperson, brand, etc. Breaking that trust can lead to a long-term negative view of the company. Not being able to back up the scarcity claim, having a questionable business reputation, and overusing a scarcity appeal can all cause scarcity to be viewed as a sales tactic.

## WHEN INFORMATION IS INCONSISTENT
## WITH CLAIMS OF SCARCITY

A business's messaging must be consistent, meaning if a limited-time offer is given, it should be for a specific number of hours, days, or weeks. Or as another example, if limited inventory is advertised, that inventory should truly be limited.

One of my students, Erica, recounted her experience with a website that sold beauty products. She purchased a limited-edition beauty piece that she had been eyeing ever since she saw it advertised on Instagram. The night she made her purchase, the beauty company had a message under the product that said "Only 1 left" in bright red font. You couldn't miss it. After Erica made her purchase, out of curiosity, she refreshed the product page on her web browser. While she expected to see a message that said "Sold Out," she instead read a message that said "Only 3 left." This prompted Erica to dig deeper into what was happening. How could there be more product available when she just bought the last one? Maybe there was a glitch with the e-commerce website or people were returning their products, she thought to herself. Erica went to the company's Twitter account to see if there were any comments that the limited-edition beauty piece was sold out. It turns out several people had inquired about the availability of the product, and the company had responded each time that there were only a few pieces left. Those messages spanned over a two-week period, which made Erica believe the scarcity claims were false, and she vowed never to buy from that company again. What Erica experienced has a technical term: "scarcity disconfirmation."

Scarcity disconfirmation occurs when the information provided to us is inconsistent with the scarcity claim a business is making—and it can be extremely detrimental to a business. In our example above, the e-commerce store advertised a "limited quantity," but that didn't line up with what customers were able to see on the website. If a store claims that the inventory of a certain product is low but the shelves are fully stocked, scarcity could be disconfirmed. The same would be true if a business promoted an exclusive membership that was actually open to anyone. In both instances, the business's reputation would suffer, and sometimes that would last permanently. Why? Because when we as consumers become distrustful, we share our distrust with others, resulting in a potentially substantial—and negative—impact on the business.

In Erica's situation, the scarcity claim was not consistent with what she saw on the website after refreshing her browser, nor with what she read on social media. Right after she figured out what happened, she went to Reddit and aired her frustration with the company. That post generated a lot of buzz and comments from other customers. While the extent to which customers decided not to purchase from the company based on Erica's post is not known, there was still some negative impact on the company's reputation.

## BRAND REPUTATION

Every experience with a business contributes to our perception of it. If we feel manipulated or lied to, not only will we not buy the company's products, but we will also warn other customers to do the same. As a business, if your customers feel tricked in any way, you will not only lose the sale; you will also lose credibility and harm your reputation.

My friend Scott told a story about how he went from taking advantage of an online promotion to completely distrusting the company. He was prepared to buy a backpack on a website he found after doing a Google search. He wasn't very familiar with the e-commerce site, but he was drawn in by the 25 percent off promotion. Scott spent about 20 minutes perusing the inventory of backpacks on the site before deciding on the one that best suited his needs. He added the backpack to his shopping cart and proceeded through the checkout process. When he reached the field to add a promo code, he copied the 25 percent off code into the box and then hit "apply." To his surprise, a red error message appeared stating that the offer was not valid for his purchase. He went back to read the fine print of the offer, and there was an abnormally long list of brands that were excluded from the offer, including the brand of backpack he had selected. He felt tricked by the company and decided against making his purchase. He ended up finding a different website that also had a percentage-off offer, but without the lengthy brand restrictions. When Scott shared this story with me, he described being turned off to the e-commerce company, and his disdain for the company was apparent.

In general, brand reputation can also impact whether or not we trust the scarcity message the company is advertising. If a company has a poor reputation, it doesn't matter if that company promotes a product or service that is actually scarce; we won't believe it either way. The same is true if the identical scarcity appeal is repeated frequently by the same company, but this time we will view the scarcity claim as manipulative.

## PROMOTION FREQUENCY

Another blatant sales tactic to use sparingly and with caution is promotion frequency. This next example is about a young girl named Mia who lived in Southern California. Although she was only 17 years old, by all accounts Mia was a responsible teenager. She worked part-time after school and earned good grades. She had even managed to save some money that she planned to use to attend college. On one July afternoon, Mia and her friends headed to Laguna Beach. After sitting on the beach for a couple of hours, the teens headed to some nearby shops to get lunch and walk around. To Mia's surprise and delight, a new clothing store had just opened, and everything was 50 percent off. A sign indicated the sale was only for a "limited time" even though it neglected to advertise a specific start or end date.

Regardless, Mia felt the urgency to buy some clothing—in fact, a lot of it—while the sale was going on. She ended up spending a week's worth of her wages in a couple of hours. Feeling a tad guilty, she justified her purchases because of the "limited-time" offer.

The next week, Mia wandered up to the Laguna Beach shops again after a morning spent with friends at the ocean. To her surprise, the sale was still going on. Mia felt that same impulse and urgency to buy again. This time, she had to use some of the savings she had put aside for college. Again, she rationalized her decision as justified given the "limited-time" sale. It wasn't until two weeks later that she noticed that the store was still having the same sale, leaving Mia to learn a lesson the hard way: that "discounted" in this case really just meant that the clothing was simply marked up and then down. She felt disappointed in herself for falling for the sales tactic and never visited the store again. In fact, she told everyone she knew about the store's "manipulation," as she put it. She was disappointed in herself, but the store lost potential sales and long-term customers. This was a clear case of overusing scarcity, and it definitely backfired.

When we're frequently exposed to a company's advertisements that emphasize some sort of restriction—a limited sale, limited quantity, limited edition—we recognize that the scarcity is not real, especially if the advertisements run for years at a time. For example, Black Angus Steakhouse is known for promoting "Dinner for Two" offers. Just like other coupons, the offer always had a specific expiration date. However, the steakhouse ran this similar promotion for so long, that customers started to just wait for the next coupon to come out. The scarcity, or limited-time offer, didn't feel so special. When a promotion is used too frequently, it can cause unintended consequences for the company.

In fact, research related to frequency and scarcity shows that companies with greater frequency of promotion are often viewed as having a lower reference price.[14] In the Black Angus example, the risk with the similar "Dinner for Two" offer is that customers would begin to use that discounted price as a reference for what the meal should cost. They would potentially value the dinner at $49.98 instead of the regular price of $66. One team of researchers conducted in-depth interviews of customers and discovered that people make inferences about seller behavior regarding price promotions and long-term patterns of promotions, and those inferences impact what the customer knows and anticipates about the brand.[15]

In addition to the perils of promotion frequency, the amount of discount offered in a promotion can also hurt sales. One study found that consumers infer information about a brand or product from price promotion patterns.[16] The study results suggested that consumers believe that higher, more constant prices are an indicator of quality, while deep discounts reflect that something might be wrong with the brand or product. So while promotions, which are a form of scarcity, can be effective, it's also important to avoid overuse and too deep of discounts to achieve long-term success.

Another thing we need to consider is whether scarcity works on everyone. In the upcoming chapters, the types of scarcity and the people they apply to are discussed in depth. However, before we consider those factors, there is another factor that must be addressed regarding consumers and their susceptibility to scarcity, and that is age.

## CUSTOMER AGE

Although we have heavily explored how scarcity impacts our decisions and purchasing behavior, scarcity doesn't have the same level of effect on everyone. Age plays a significant role in how we will respond to a signal that a product or service is scarce. Therefore, the age of the targeted customer group is something that must be evaluated before using scarcity—specifically goals and how decisions are made.

The older we get, the more we are aware of the time we have left in life. Consequently, older consumers (65 years and older) are generally not as concerned about the future as adults who are younger than they are, and they are also not as focused on competitive goals.[17] Instead, they shift their attention to emotionally meaningful goals, such as deepening close relationships, cherishing the present, and pursuing positive life experiences. Goals aren't the only thing that changes when it comes to age either. The way information is processed and the way decisions are made also shift.[18]

As consumers get older, they start to process information differently than do their younger counterparts. They are typically not in the same social environments as they were previously, such as working full-time and interacting with coworkers. Their social circle becomes smaller. Additionally, their media patterns change.

Instead of choosing media based on entertainment, they put a greater emphasis on information value. They are more cautious when making decisions and prefer more time to process information than younger consumers. Some experiments have shown that it is not just a preference for more time to process information, but a necessity.[19] When we get older, our ability to process information slows down—we can still interpret information and make decisions, but we can't do it at the same pace as when we were younger. We require more time. Consequently, we adopt certain strategies to help us.

Because older consumers have a harder time processing information than when they were younger, they rely on their experience. We see this play out with brand and/or product loyalty. The older people get, the more loyal they become to certain brands and do not become swayed by others just because something is promoted as scarce. In fact, if they're satisfied with a product, they will commit to buying that same product again in the future.[20]

A 2021 survey supports this concept by showing the difference in brand loyalty among the various generations and the likelihood to try new products based on age. The survey results showed that 49 percent of Gen Z respondents reported that they repeatedly buy the same product if they find one they like, but that number went up substantially with each generational cohort. For example, 59 percent of millennials, 67 percent of Gen Xers, and 75 percent of boomers said they would continue to buy the same product.[21]

Outside of experience, there are other tactics older consumers use when making purchase decisions, too.[22] For instance, older consumers will adopt strategies to cope with the limited cognitive resources and information load. For example, they will quickly eliminate as many alternatives as they possibly can to reduce information overload.[23] If they are presented with something that is undesirable about a product (e.g., it's scarce), that will be used as a reason to eliminate that option from further consideration.[24] From a marketing perspective, this suggests that older consumers would not be as easily swayed by a scarcity message unless it has a direct impact on their decision.

In the context of advertisements, older consumers are more likely to recall a slogan promising some type of emotional reward than one promising some other type of reward. One study found that older adults preferred an advertisement for a camera that stated, "Capture those special moments," over an identical ad, but with the line, "Capture the unexplored world."[25] Therefore, if a product is geared to an older age bracket, such as a three-week European cruise, it is best not to push a scarcity message about rooms booking up quickly or the exclusivity of the ship. Instead, it is better to highlight the experience the older travelers will have on the cruise and the memories they will make. Most likely, those consumers just won't care about scarcity, and those overt attempts to influence can turn them off.

---

As the research and lessons learned from other companies have shown us in this chapter, when scarcity is made up or used as an obvious sales tactic, it can turn customers away. Remember that businesses must be truthful and consistent in how they use scarcity, because there is the risk of not only losing the sale, but also harming their reputation.

In the next few chapters, we will explore specific types of scarcity messages and how to use them effectively and ethically.

## KEY SELLING POINTS

- Artificial scarcity occurs when the quantity of an item is intentionally restricted, even though there could be enough of that item to meet demand. It can also mean that there is an implied limitation.

- When scarcity is viewed as a sales tactic, it can backfire. Consumers want to feel as though they can trust the salesperson, brand, etc.

- Scarcity disconfirmation occurs when the information provided to us is inconsistent with the scarcity claim a business is making—and it can be extremely detrimental to a business.

- It is OK to highlight the scarcity of a product, service, etc., as long as it's honest and helpful.

- Since age plays a significant role in how consumers will respond to a signal that a product or service is scarce, it should be considered before using scarcity in a marketing message.

# PART TWO

# USING SCARCITY

# CHAPTER 6

# "Time Is Running Out!"

"Look Who's Back! McDonald's Shamrock Shake Returns to Mark the First Green of Spring" read the headline of a 2021 press release.[1] Each year, much anticipation builds as customers await the limited-time release of the green milkshake from McDonald's that has become a cult classic and represents the "greening of spring." A menu item that was conceived in 1967 by Connecticut McDonald's owner and operator Hal Rosen to celebrate St. Patrick's Day has become a global sensation and was also used in part to fund the first Ronald McDonald House in 1974.

How has the Shamrock Shake remained popular nearly 50 years after its inception? There is no doubt that the tastiness and marketing promotions behind the seasonal drink are factors in its success, but that's not what pushed the drink to legend status. We have time-related scarcity to thank for that.

During my conversation with Dean Barrett, retired McDonald's Senior Vice President of Global Marketing who worked for the company for 41 years, he explained just how McDonald's uses limited-time offerings to develop brand affinity and loyalty, while at the same time cultivating customer interaction.

McDonald's has a 60-year history of doing things fun and exciting and creating trends that connect to how people live and what's going on around them, whether that be food (e.g., the Shamrock Shake) or limited-time promotions tied to big events, such as sports events or major movie releases around the world. Having the opportunity to do limited-time offers for customers has become part of the brand's culture. McDonald's uses limited-time products to surprise and delight customers. "By doing so, I think McDonald's gains greater brand loyalty and more repeat visits. I also believe it's how McDonald's builds deeper and strong relationships with customers over the long term," explained Barrett.

For the company, limited-time offers are not about the spur-of-the-moment "How much can I sell?" but instead "How can I connect customers with the brand and become part of the culture?" This approach leads to lasting brand affinity and a connection with customers' lives. It has allowed McDonald's to create culturally relevant moments.

McDonald's is intentional with the release of limited-time offers, which the company bases on what customers are craving at the time or what they have craved in the past. If a previous limited-time offering was popular among customers, McDonald's considers bringing it back and, in many cases, has brought back time and again. However, the limited-time offering might be removed after a period of time to continue to surprise customers and lead to some fun (*hint:* remember the McRib fans from Chapter 1?). In a way, the sporadic market release leads to a treasure hunt for fans.

From Barrett's perspective, "I believe that because McDonald's brings products in and out over time, that it is therefore able to create that long-term brand affinity and brand strength." Plus everyone gets to have a little fun. McDonald's keeps customers guessing about, and even demanding, the release of the McRib, their favorite Chicken McNugget flavor, or the Shamrock Shake.

Even if a business doesn't have a marketing budget as large as McDonald's has, the same principles can be applied to its products and services. A product or service bundle can be turned into a limited-time item that is released only certain times of the year. Are you someone who loves the fall season? Limited-time pumpkin spice items will allow you to express your love for all things autumn-related.

## SCARCITY THROUGH TIME RESTRICTIONS

"Enroll now for only $1. Offer ends soon!" This was on a sandwich board in the parking lot of a local gym near my house, and is a perfect example of how time pressure can lead to sales.

Just as quantities can be limited and lead to scarcity, so can a restriction on time. Amazon uses this tactic with its lightning deals. Not only do you see the number of discounted products already claimed by other shoppers, but there is also a countdown timer showing you how many hours or minutes you have until the offer is gone . . . forever.

Time-related scarcity is best used for nonconspicuous goods, which are those that provide some type of utility or benefit and are not used to show status and wealth. For example, aluminum foil, microwaves, and toothpaste would all fall into this category. Even for these mundane products, our brains are still activated if there is a presence of time-related scarcity.

# IN A TIME CRUNCH

Studies have shown that when we feel pressured to make a decision, the amount of information we are able to process diminishes. We focus on features that can be rapidly and effortlessly evaluated.[2] When the available time to complete a task is believed to be insufficient, feelings of stress kick in. Think about the last time you were under time pressure to complete a project, or think back to your days in school when you waited until the last minute to finish an assignment. We feel a level of stress in these situations. The same thing happens with limited-time offers.

When we perceive a lack of time, the related stress influences our decisions. Research has shown that as consumers, we are sensitive to a promotion's deadline, and that time pressure can increase our intention to buy the promoted product or service.[3] This is especially true if we think the price of the item is going to go up. When we expect the price to increase, we buy now. On the other hand, when we expect the price to drop, we wait for the sale.[4] That's what caused Ryan to stock up on deodorant. When he came home from the store with not one stick of deodorant, but ten, his wife couldn't help but question his purchase decision. Ryan simply explained, "The deodorant was marked down by 20 percent. I didn't know when it would go on sale again, so I decided to buy ten."

Here's what happens when we are faced with a limited-time offer.

We skip the normal steps involved in making a decision to purchase something. Remember the mental shortcuts we talked about previously? That applies in a situation of time pressure. We stop looking for additional information to help us decide whether to buy something or move on. We are no longer exposed to competing products and deals because we are no longer looking.[5] Instead, we are compelled to buy right then and there. This is great for businesses. As a consumer, not only did you accelerate your purchase, but you also had limited exposure to competing products and deals. Therefore, it keeps us focused on a particular company or product. It's a win-win for marketers.

## IT DOESN'T NEED TO BE A COMPETITION

Unlike scarcity caused by popular demand, when it comes to time-based scarcity, social cues are not effective. Consumers are not in competition with each other to get the scarce item before it runs out. And unlike supply-related scarcity, where each time a customer purchases the scarce item, the remaining number of items available for purchase decreases, all a customer needs to do is purchase the item before the sale deadline in order to "win."[6] In essence, the competition is with the clock, not other people. For that reason, marketing messages that include social cues, such as "nearly sold out," are not effective. Businesses are better off avoiding social cues and instead keeping the promotional messages simple and clear by including the sale end date and future price after the sale.[7]

# LIMITED-TIME OFFERS COME IN MANY SHAPES AND SIZES

Scarcity caused by a time restriction can come in various forms—limited-time offers, flash sales, countdown timers, and coupons. Each of these techniques can be effective, as long as they are implemented correctly. Let's dive deeper into each one.

## LIMITED-TIME OFFERS

The two examples that follow involve offerings from food establishments, but certainly a business doesn't have to be a restaurant to apply a limited-time discount.

### BJ's Prime Rib Special

BJ's Restaurants, which is a publicly traded company with nearly 200 restaurants nationwide, often uses limited-time offers and discounts to boost sales. Take the Prime Rib Special offered to customers as an example. BJ's positioned the offer as follows: "For a limited time only. No promo code required. Limited quantities available."[8] For this scarcity message to work, there are a few things that must be addressed, all of which are supported by psychological research.

The most important thing is to follow certain guidelines to make the offer successful. Let's break it down using BJ's prime rib offer:

First, the limited-time discount should not be the same as a recent promotion, meaning BJ's shouldn't run a duplicate promotion on the prime rib.

Second, there must be clear guidelines given for the offer, and they must be enforced. Within the promotional message, BJ's provided details on the offer, including that it was available only on Fridays and Saturdays after 4 p.m. and all day on Sundays.

Third, the consumer must be exposed to the scarcity multiple times. BJ's promoted the Prime Rib Special on its website, on social media profiles, and within the restaurants.

Have these types of limited offers been successful for BJ's? If you track its stock price and revenue, they appear to be working. The company has experienced revenue growth year over year.

## THE PUMPKIN SPICE LATTE: THE KING OF LIMITED-TIME SEASONAL DRINKS

Starbucks often uses time-related scarcity to drive sales. Just think about the Pumpkin Spice Latte (PSL) that has cultivated a fan base who anxiously awaits its release each year. (*Note:* Starbucks has trademarked "PSL"!) The PSL is considered one of Starbucks's most popular and quintessential seasonal drinks. According to Tim Kern, who started working for Starbucks when it was a small regional chain and who stayed for 20 years, the PSL nearly didn't make it to the menu. "A number of us thought it was a beverage so dominated by a flavor other than coffee that it didn't put Starbucks' coffee in the best light," explained Kern.[9]

Let's step back in time and look at how the PSL came to be.

The Starbucks team responsible for choosing flavors went through a brainstorming process and came up with 10 product ideas. The team had customers try the new beverages, and the pumpkin drink fell into the middle of the spectrum. At the time, there weren't any drinks around pumpkin. The team decided to pursue the pumpkin idea by setting up a "liquid lab" complete with Thanksgiving-related things, including pumpkin pies, to cultivate the feelings of fall. It was the middle of January at the time.[10] The company experimented with various fall-related flavors and decided on a recipe that didn't actually have a note of pumpkin in it (for the record, there is no pumpkin in the drink at all); yet Starbucks chose to name the drink "Pumpkin Spice Latte."

In 2002, the PSL was tested in Vancouver and Washington, DC. Within one week, sales spiked and surpassed the initial projections.[11] Starbucks struggled to keep up with inventory. Ten years after its introduction to the market, Starbucks had sold roughly 200 million PSLs.[12] By 2019, the number was about 424 million worldwide.[13]

The drink that almost didn't make it to the market has become the king of limited-time seasonal drinks and has spurred a pumpkin spice movement. The craze over the PSL is a prime example of how a limited-time offering leads to the perception of scarcity. The drink is only available for a limited time each year. Customers know that they have to act before it is gone. There is also the bandwagon effect at play, which we will get into more in Chapter 9. The popularity of the PSL causes us to follow the behavior of others and get into the craze, too.

The PSL isn't an unusual occurrence for Starbucks. Even nondrink products offered as a limited edition or for a limited time fly off the shelves. Take the reusable holiday cups released each year. These fashionable cups stir up a craze come November. One article headline on ABC7.com captures the essence of the excitement among Starbucks lovers, "Attention red cup fans! Here's how to get your free reusable holiday cup at Starbucks." The reusable cups are typically given away free with the purchase of a holiday drink. The 2021 ABC7 article warned fans that while Starbucks would be giving these cups away free, it was for one day only, communicating both a limited-edition offer and a limited-time opportunity.[14]

## FLASH SALES

The September 1, 2021, headline on Adgully announced, "Five-day flash sale with savings of up to 60% for your staycation on Yas Island."[15] Yas Island (in Abu Dhabi) had released a limited-time offer, in the form of a flash sale, for local customers looking for a staycation. The offer included discounted rates of up to 60 percent off staycation packages and up to 50 percent off day tickets for theme parks and CLYMB Abu Dhabi.

Flash sales, like the one offered by Yas Island, have become a common method for businesses to quickly increase sales revenue, including the hospitality industry. I define a flash sale as a sale of particular products for a very short period of time. One study in which researchers interviewed 46 hotel managers found that flash sales were most often used during a period of need.[16] The managers that ran flash sales promotions all mentioned that this marketing tactic was best used during a time when sales were low. In each of these instances, the managers described flash sales as a means to fill rooms that would otherwise be empty.

Consequently, the managers were using these temporary price cuts to address the perishability problem of their properties. However, there were other benefits beyond inventory and revenue management.

Flash sales offered the advantage of increased brand marketing and improved customer relationships. In fact, most of the interviewees explained that flash sales have a promotional benefit to the hotels through increased exposure and advertisement of the property. For example, when a mass email promoting a flash sale is sent, information about the hotel lands in the inboxes of thousands of potential customers, thus raising awareness of the brand. One of the interviewees, a general manager of an upscale hotel in Sarasota, Florida, explained this brand promotion well: "It has been a proven message to gain exposure to a large market. So, in other words, there are a lot of people . . . even if they did not buy it, they receive your name and your location via email. And it certainly . . . for those people that may know of Sarasota, but did not know what hotels were in Sarasota, our name is there on it. So, for future use they might look at it."[17]

Airlines employ similar tactics with the use of flash sales. Fox News ran a story in 2011 featuring an interview with an anonymous airline revenue manager. Each airline employs a group of revenue managers who are responsible for maximizing profits by adjusting airfares throughout the day, based on route, season, demand, supply, and other variables. Although airline ticket prices are not always touted as flash sales, the way in which the prices are adjusted still align with this tactic. Airlines use computer systems and algorithms to determine what prices to offer, at what intervals, and in what quantity. The anonymous airline revenue manager explained the following to Fox News:

The computer knows that, by releasing (for example) five seats at a very low price, ten seats at a slightly higher price, and twenty seats at a slightly higher price, it can maximize revenue as the flight fills up. On a full flight, we no longer want to offer that el-cheapo fare because it is based on supply and demand. The computer adjusts fares all the way up until the departure time, but as a revenue manager, I can go in and adjust things based on information that the computer may not know. For example, are there specific events taking place at a destination? Are there certain conditions at the departure airport that will allow more than the desired amount of seats to go empty such as weather?[18]

Similar to the hotel managers, airline revenue managers utilize temporary price cuts as a way to boost the sales of an otherwise perishable product. Flash sales are not just beneficial for hotels and airlines, though; many other companies have benefited from the use of this form of limited-time offer. J Crew offered a one-day flash sale that included 60 percent off sales items by using a particular promo code.[19] Kohl's periodically offers discounts for reward members only, such as "an extra 20 percent off, today only." Best Buy offers "flash" discounts to email subscribers. Amazon regularly releases "Lightning Deals." Pier One Imports sends Flash Sale Friday emails promoting temporary sales.

## THE DAILY DEAL

Flash sales came on to the retail scene in 2004 through the website Woot.com, which focused on daily deals and is considered one of the pioneers of this model of selling online.[20] Every day, customers were given a 24-hour window to take advantage of a promoted deal. The model was simple. Each day, a new item was promoted with the same 24-hour deadline to purchase. The range of products varied from consumer goods to electronics. At its peak, Woot.com was attracting 5 million visitors to its site every month.[21] During the 2008 financial crisis in the United States, flash sales and daily deals kept many brick-and-mortar businesses afloat. While websites offering daily deals still exist, including Woot.com (which was purchased by Amazon in 2010 for $110 million), these types of promotions have been adopted by many businesses both online and offline.

When creating a flash sale, there are some things to keep in mind. Generally, 24- to 72-hour flash sales are ideal in creating urgency without irritating customers because they did not see the sale in time. If the sale is offered online, it should be during the time of day people are most often on the site. For example, if website traffic is highest in the evenings, then that is when the flash sale should start. The flash sale should not be complicated. If customers are given too many options or choices, it makes the offer confusing (e.g., 10 percent off when you spend $100, 20 percent off when you spend $200, 30 percent off when you spend $300 . . .).

Although Trader Joe's doesn't offer flash sales, the company is great at limiting choices, which in turns simplifies the shopping experience and is a good example to follow when considering how to set up a sale. Trader Joe's purposely limits the number of items displayed. A *Business Insider* reporter compared Trader Joe's product stock with the stock carried by a neighborhood grocery store.[22] Reporter Jack Houston counted 144 pasta sauces, 44 olive oils, and 172 cereals at the local grocery store. The nearby Trader Joe's, however, only stocked 14 pasta sauces, 14 olive oils, and 39 cereals. Less choice has been a key to Trader Joe's success. Trader Joe's has continuously ranked number one in customer preference, and when calculating sales based on square footage, Trader Joe's outperforms its competitors.

To sum up: As we have seen, many types of businesses can benefit from a flash sale. If trying to move a particular product or increase interest in a service, a business can schedule and promote a sale that lasts a very short period of time. In the example of the hotel managers, a business holding this type of sale can increase brand awareness and strengthen relationships with customers through the offering of the flash sale and the marketing communication that would go along with it.

## COUNTDOWN TIMERS

James was lying in bed one night and casually shopping online. He added a few items to his shopping cart when suddenly he noticed a countdown timer appear indicating that the items would only stay in his shopping cart for a limited time. His heart started to race, and as the time ticked down, he also forgot what other items he needed. He just knew he would remember right before he fell asleep. So James began panic buying by adding anything and everything he could think of to his shopping cart. With

15 minutes still to go, he felt like he was in a race against the clock. Literally.

Countdown timers are reminders that many e-commerce websites employ to tell us that our time to take advantage of a current offer, free shipping, or a sale is limited. The clock counting down creates urgency and anticipated regret if we don't act quickly. These timers appear on website banners and emails for sales, offers, and free shipping.

To further create the feeling of FOMO, many businesses show a message after the timer has finished letting customers know that the sale or special offer has expired. Remember that we have a greater fear of what we might lose than what we might gain. Therefore, the next time we see a countdown timer, we will remember that feeling of loss we experienced when we realized we missed the previous sale—and this time we'll take action to ensure we don't lose again.

If you have an e-commerce business, why not test a countdown timer? It is an easy way to create urgency.

## COUPONS

Coupons are one of the oldest marketing tools used by companies. Coupon offers have been around for centuries. In the late nineteenth century, Coca-Cola Co.'s founder, Asa Candler, mailed handwritten tickets offering a free glass of soda to people who lived nearby the pharmacies that he supplied with his syrup.[23] Coupons are just as effective and enticing today as they were then.

Here is some proof.

Coupons.com had an average of 3.3 million unique visitors each month throughout 2020.[24] That's a lot of people looking for coupons! That same year, nearly $189 billion in coupons was offered in the United States alone by 3,282 manufacturers.[25] But how many people actually used these coupons? It is estimated that 52 million Americans redeemed mobile coupons, and that doesn't even include print coupon redemptions![26] What's even more astonishing is that online coupon users, on average, spend 24 percent more than regular shoppers, and 74 percent of consumers follow brands on social media to look for coupons.[27] Anyone have a coupon?

People like coupons. Just think about the popular reality television show *Extreme Couponing*, where each episode focuses on a shopper who uses coupons to save hundreds, if not thousands, of dollars on purchases. During one episode, J'aime Kirlew from Bethesda, Maryland, packed her shopping cart with 62 bottles of French's mustard and then proclaimed, "I don't even eat mustard."[28] By the time all her items, including 100 yogurt cups, 35 cans of soup, 40 boxes of cereal, and 90 packages of cold cuts, were scanned by the cashier, she had reached a whopping total of $1,902.63. After handing over her coupons, the new total was $103.72. While this example might be "extreme," there is a psychological explanation regarding the attraction to coupons.

Coupons make us happy. At least that's what one study conducted by a professor of neuroeconomics and his team found when analyzing how a $10 coupon affected people while grocery shopping online.[29] Half of the participants were given the $10 coupon, and the other half were not. The impact of the coupons was then measured through various means, including level of hormones in the blood, cardiac activity, mood, respiration, and perspiration. According to the study, our oxytocin, which is associated with love and happiness, significantly increases when we receive a coupon. What is even more intriguing is that the oxytocin level spikes more with coupons than when we kiss, cuddle, or even receive a gift! Our stress level also decreases. Basically, we become happier and more relaxed. As Professor Zak, the lead researcher, explained, "These results, combined with the findings of other research, suggest that coupons can directly impact happiness of people, promote positive health and increase the ability to handle stressful situations."[30]

It is no wonder that marketers have been using coupons for decades to attract new customers and promote new product lines. Coupons are also one of the most common types of time-related scarcity. Coupons cause happiness and less stress when we first get the offers because they elicit potential gain. As we explored in Chapter 4, though, coupons create a fear of loss.[31]

The duration of the coupon, meaning the time period between when the coupon is released and when it expires, has been known to impact the effectiveness of the offer. For instance, if the number of potential customers redeeming the coupon is large, a shorter coupon duration will drive higher profit.[32] Urgency declines with a longer time limit for the offer or coupon. However, there are trade-offs when it comes to choosing an expiration date. Longer expiration periods give customers more time to become aware of the offer but create the risk of customers forgetting about the offer or delaying their decision.[33] On the other side, shorter expiration periods can increase the sense of urgency to take action but can be perceived as inconvenient.[34] So where does that leave marketers in terms of figuring out an expiration period? One study concluded that a time limit less than two weeks maximizes the success of the coupon.[35] The time limit is something that must be tested by marketing managers.

This scenario can be seen in manufacturer coupons versus store coupons. Manufacturer coupons tend to have a lengthy expiration date, and there is typically a sharp redemption rate right before the coupon expires. Store coupons, on the other hand, tend to have a much shorter window and do not give shoppers the luxury of waiting too long to buy a product and redeem the offer. As shoppers, we are strongly motivated to buy now. If the coupon offer allows, we often buy more than we would have otherwise.

## IT'S PERSONAL

The rise of digital coupons has been a trend throughout the years, and the pandemic that began in 2020 only accelerated it. One of the major benefits of digital coupons, outside the fact that you don't have to cut through paper and hope you remember the cutout coupon when you shop next, is that digital coupons have become highly personalized. With digital coupons, you can target customers based on their purchase history *and* segment the offers provided.

Kohl's, an omnichannel retailer that has more than 1,100 stores in 49 states, is a great example of a business implementing personalization into its promotion strategy. Over the last several years, Kohl's has been using its customer data to increase sales. Through Kohl's digital wallet, credit card, and loyalty program, Kohl's has been able to offer personalized deals both digitally and through direct mail campaigns. "Loyalty is very important. Longer term, personalization is probably more important because [it] has a big impact around the effectiveness of our marketing and driving more traffic into the stores," explained Kohl's CEO Kevin Mansell.

During the first year of personalized marketing, Kohl's goal was to develop 5 million personalized touches.[36] Kohl's has since expanded its approach to personalization through in-store Wi-Fi. When shoppers log onto the store's Wi-Fi system, Kohl's can collect data to determine their shopping patterns.[37] This data also allows Kohl's to determine in real time whether to provide a personalized offer based on a person's shopping habits.

Dunkin' Donuts, self-proclaimed as "the world's leading baked goods and coffee chain," uses digital coupons to entice customers to come back.[38] When customers download the Dunkin' app, which they are incentivized to do for a discount, the company can monitor their activity, including if they return to one of its stores.[39] Then Dunkin' sends the customers more deals to get them to buy more, and you can even earn free drinks by coming back and earning points.

Artificial intelligence (AI), specifically chatbot technology, has allowed companies to get even more personalized with their offers. Chatbots interact with customers in real time and can monitor the customer's online activity. By identifying the customer's intent, online behavior, and interests, AI technology can develop personalized online coupons that can be redeemed in store or online.[40]

There are a few things to keep in mind when a business decides to implement coupons as a time-related scarcity tactic. First and foremost, the message needs to be clear (e.g., "20% off your entire order"). Second, there needs to be a time restraint to create urgency (e.g., "20% off your entire order . . . offer expires 1/31"). Third, the coupon must get in front of customers, which could mean digital coupons offered on the website, shared through social media, or sent via email. Direct mail and newspaper inserts are also viable ways to distribute coupons. Finally, avoid offering the same coupons repeatedly. Doing so will diminish the value of the product and/or brand.

One customer, Barbara, described her perception of a local restaurant and its steak dinner offer. According to Barbara, the restaurant regularly released a coupon for its three-course steak dinner. "If I don't have the coupon, I won't go to the restaurant. Why would I pay full price? The dinner is worth the amount of the coupon in my opinion."

Groupon is one of the best examples of a company that has figured out time-related scarcity using coupons. The coupon giant, which is essentially the intermediary between customers and local businesses, advertises special offers for brick-and-mortar companies.

Each offer on the platform has a stated end date found in the fine print section.

Additionally, Groupon runs other promotions that allow consumers to get an even higher discount, such as 20 percent off the Groupon price. Groupon uses push notifications, emails, and messages within the mobile app to get this information in front of customers.

Take the following as additional examples of companies using coupons effectively. Note that each of these offers included a coupon code and expiration date.

- **TrueShip.** "Limited-Time Sale: 50% off First Month of ReadyShipper Shipping Software for New Users with Coupon Code RS-SAVE-5"[41]

- **Nissan of Victoria.** "$30 off an air conditioning service"[42]

- **BlueHost.** "Just $3.95 per Month, a Limited Time Offer"[43]

- **Dell.** "Save $150 on XPS, Alienware, Inspiron"[44]

- **Jo-Ann Stores.** "Time is ticking . . . these deals are gone tomorrow!"[45]

- **J. Crew.** "For a Limited Time, Rewards Members Get 2X Points on Purchases (and Free Shipping Always)!"[46]

Time-related scarcity has proved effective in increasing sales and attracting customers. Yet when trying to reach customers who value exclusivity, another type of scarcity would be more beneficial. The next chapter explores how supply-related scarcity is attractive to those who want to be different and stand out from others.

## KEY SELLING POINTS

- Time-related scarcity is best used for nonconspicuous goods, which are those that provide some type of utility or benefit and are not used to show status and wealth.

- When we perceive a lack of time, the related stress influences our decisions.

- When it comes to time-based scarcity, social cues are not effective. Consumers are not in competition with each other to get the scarce item before it runs out.

- All a customer needs to do is purchase the item before the sale deadline in order to "win," so in essence the competition is with the clock, not other people.

- The promotional messages should be kept simple and clear by including the sale end date and future price after the sale.

- Scarcity caused by a time restriction can come in many forms—from limited time offers, flash sales, countdown timers, or coupons.

# CHAPTER 7

# You Are Special

IT WAS RATED THE number one restaurant in London. Over one long weekend, there were 116 missed calls from patrons trying to book their reservation for the "appointment-only" eatery. On one day alone, the restaurant's listing received 89,000 views on TripAdvisor.[1] The reviews were fantastic. People commented about the difficulty of getting a table reserved but raved about the food. Some of the reviews mentioned that it was well worth the wait. There was no question that the appointment-only restaurant was exclusive. The only thing was, the restaurant did not exist.

It started out as an experiment that was meant to answer the question, "Could a fake restaurant become a top-rated establishment on TripAdvisor?" According to the mastermind behind the experiment, who goes by the name Oobah Butler, "With the help of fake reviews, mystique, and nonsense," the answer is yes—and The Shed at Dulwich proved it.[2]

Butler used his home, which was really a shed in a south London garden, as the location of the restaurant (hence the name "The Shed at Dulwich"). He purchased a $13 burner phone and provided only the road of his shed as the main address. Butler created his listing on TripAdvisor and forged ahead with the development of a restaurant website, Theshedatdulwich.com. He needed a catchy menu and decided to name all the dishes after moods, such as Lust, Love, Empathetic, Contemplation, Comfort, and Happy. However, he needed photos to go along with his menu, so he created images of appealing dishes using props to mimic food, including bleach tablets, sponges and shaving cream. After uploading all the information to TripAdvisor, he got the official email that his listing request was approved.

The Shed at Dulwich was initially ranked 18,149 on TripAdvisor in the list of London restaurants. Butler knew that he needed reviews to push the listing up in rank, but there was TripAdvisor's spam technology to overcome. So Butler focused on getting reviews written by real people (his friends and acquaintances) on various computers to avoid spam detection. Within two weeks, the restaurant listing had moved up to the top 10,000 on TripAdvisor. Then the strangest thing happened. Remember the burner phone? It began to ring. Startled, Butler answered the phone. The person on the other end was inquiring about how to get a reservation booked. Out of panic, Butler responded that the restaurant was booked for the next six weeks and hung up the phone. His phone continued to vibrate with messages from people trying to reserve their tables. One request was for a reservation of nine people in four months. The emails started to flood in for appointment requests, too. The Shed at Dulwich moved up to position 1,456 on TripAdvisor. Butler continued to receive calls and messages from customers scrambling to get their reservations.

Then Butler started to receive free samples in the mail from companies vying for his business (they had to estimate his location). A production company, publicist, and even government council all tried to get in touch with Butler as the news of his exclusive restaurant spread. Eventually, The Shed at Dulwich moved to number 30 of the top restaurants in London.

If that wasn't enough to digest, what happened next is almost unbelievable. Butler decided to open his fake restaurant to the public.

This was no easy endeavor. He had to stage his shed and garden to look like a restaurant and needed to have food to serve. He recruited a friend as his chef for the night, and they concocted a menu based on $1 frozen dinners. Butler also asked other friends to act as restaurant patrons while real guests dined. He even brought in a waitress to serve his guests.

The first two guests arrived—a couple from California who were in London for a Pokémon convention. They were served a spruced-up plate of macaroni and cheese. The woman took out her phone to snap a picture of the food but after looking through her camera put it away without taking the picture. After 40 minutes, the couple left, and the man looked angry. That might not seem shocking for the $1 frozen dinners from the fake restaurant, but the response from another group of customers was unexpected.

After various tables of real customers had been served throughout the night, a table of four got up to leave. Butler walked the group out of the restaurant and apologized, saying that the menus were new and providing other excuses. During his apology, he was interrupted by someone in the foursome. She wanted to know if it would be easier to get into the restaurant now that she and her friends had been there once. They would like to come back again. This left Butler temporarily speechless.

Butler walked back to the shed to share the news with his friends. That is when the stand-in waitress informed them that the overall feedback from the customers was excellent.

While this story is a bit shocking and funny, what happened isn't surprising. At least not when you consider the power of scarcity. Although Butler's experiment was to see if he could get a fake restaurant to become top-rated on TripAdvisor, his application of the scarcity principle is what fueled his success. By making the restaurant exclusive and difficult to get into, he created a sense of urgency and persistence among customers. Through the "by appointment only" model and the reviews that communicated the difficulty of making a reservation, the value of the restaurant went up in customers' minds. Remember, though, it didn't work on all his customers. The California couple wasn't impressed by the "quality" of the food, but other customers wanted to make sure they would be able to come back.

When it comes to scarcity, something that has a limited or restricted supply is appealing to people who are looking for prestige, respect, or uniqueness. Economic, sociological, and psychological studies have been devoted to the explanation of the feelings evoked by owning a scarce item. For instance, the possession of a scarce item can be a source of status or power and has been known to boost self-image.[3] People often seek out self-expression through possessions and want to be envied and admired. That is why many of us are drawn to exclusive goods, fast fashion, or events with limited ticket availability. Not only do we want to keep up with the Joneses; we want to feel that we are different from them, in a good way. Within psychology circles, this concept falls under the umbrella of social comparison theory. According to this theory, we determine our individual value by comparing ourselves with others. We relate our qualities to the qualities of the people we meet.[4] We continually compare ourselves with hypothetical neighbors regarding material wealth and appearance.[5] And that is why there are stories of real neighbors competing during the holidays to have the most fantastic and memorable decorated home.[6]

Luxury retailers are great at capitalizing on exclusivity and cultivating the perception that if you own something that is rare and special, you must also be rare and special. Companies also provide exclusive invitations, special privileges, and access to events that are reserved for their top customers. American Express has airport lounges reserved for its top cardholders, and Gucci invites its top customers to the Cannes Film Festival.[7] Nordstrom also harnesses the power of exclusivity by providing its top rewards club members early access to events. All these examples work because of scarcity. Even in today's age when everything is available at our fingertips, we still want to feel like we have something no one else has.

## ADDRESSING THE NEED FOR UNIQUENESS

Are you a coffee snob? Although many of us drink coffee because of the caffeine and taste, some of us only drink rare blends of coffee in an effort to distinguish ourselves as a coffee connoisseur. It's the same thing with wine and even craft beers. We want to set ourselves apart and be viewed as unique. If this behavior describes you, then a product that is in limited supply is especially attractive. Less is definitely more for you.

As we have seen, a limited or restricted supply can also come in the form of invitations, privileges, events, or services, and suggests that fewer people will have access. Why is this so effective?

Sometimes we just want to be different from everyone else, which is known as the *need for uniqueness*. Social psychology theories have identified uniqueness as one of the key factors that we desire and want to maintain.[8] We seek uniqueness in socially approved ways, as in the example of our coffee connoisseurs. It is also why some of us may be willing to pay anywhere from $40,000 to $500,000 for one of the few Birkin bags created by Hermès.

While the need for uniqueness is stronger in some people than others, it's especially prevalent within Western society where the overall desire is to be different. If your customers have a high need for uniqueness, offering a limited-time price promotion is not going to be as effective as having special invitations, events, and sales. These customers will also be less likely to choose a popular alternative if a product is not available. It's not always easy to determine whether customers have a strong need for uniqueness or not, but plenty of research has shown that anything associated with conspicuous consumption tends to do well when scarcity is applied. Products and services associated with conspicuous consumption are those that display wealth or status, such as luxury goods, automobiles, and high-end electronics and services (private chef, anyone?). These are products and services that our family members, friends, and acquaintances can see us use. Owning a guitar that sold out at the store because it was on sale doesn't satisfy the need for uniqueness—but owning a guitar handcrafted by a company that produces a limited number each year does.

Although candy is not an item associated with conspicuous consumption, one scarcity study used this product category to establish the effectiveness of restricted supply. When the study participants were told there was limited availability of the candy, it caused them to eat more of it and increased their desire to buy the candy. That finding is not particularly surprising. What was surprising though was that participants said they were willing to pay more for the candy.[9] This finding suggests that companies shouldn't feel pressured to discount a product when they have limited availability; in fact it actually supports raising prices instead. In the end, companies can make more money by selling fewer units of whatever it is they're selling.

Scarcity messages that use limited supply or exclusivity are designed to make us feel that certain items are special, resulting in a feeling of distinctiveness, but these messages must be made in a way that suggests there is a limited supply versus low quantity due to popular demand. A high level of demand suggests that the product is *popular* rather than *exclusive*, which means owning the product does not satisfy our need for uniqueness but instead counteracts it. We would value a product less when more people own it.[10] Limited supply also creates communities. Take Harry & David as an example, because it has been successful at building community one product at a time.

Harry & David has a nearly 100-year history of providing fresh fruit and hand-picked gifts. The company, which was first known for its delicious pears, has since substantially grown its product line. What has been constant is the company's sense of community, not to mention its offering of unique fruit—ranging from exquisite grapes to delicious peaches—and other gourmet gifts. Most recently, though, the subcommunities among Harry & David's customers have taken off, fueled by exclusivity and limited supply.

When I first interviewed Jim McCann, the founder of 1-800-Flowers.com which also owns Harry & David, he shared a story that caught my attention because it related perfectly to what I had come to realize about scarcity. Exclusive access and limited-supply products attract our attention and spur our desires. That is what happened at Harry & David.

Harry & David has been providing products from what it considers to be the best growers and producers around the country, a group the company calls its Artisan Select, which is something customers know and love. But as Harry & David has come to realize, some products that are "the best of the best" are only available in very limited quantities. So limited, in fact, that Harry & David really can't offer them on its very popular website. There just isn't enough product to go around. That is where the idea of subcommunities started to take form. The team at Harry & David knew that there was a subset of the community who would like to engage more and is interested in certain product categories, whether that's baked goods or unique produce, and the company took great steps to cater to this segment with extraordinary finds. This story of butter explains how.

Harry & David invites customers to sign up for an email and/or text list based on their specific interests so that they will be notified when Harry & David comes across a special find. Customers are informed of these special lists, or communities, through Jim's weekly newsletter that reaches about 7.5 million readers and through a direct email campaign sent to people based on their shopping patterns. The communities have a limit to how many members can join, which is clearly communicated. For instance, an email may notify customers that there's a certain interest-based community with 11 people now and a cap of 25 members. That community will be alerted when there is a new find that meets their interests, and this is exactly where and how one group of customers found out about hard-to-get butter.

There's a woman who makes butter for 10 of the finest restaurants in the country. Her capacity is limited, and therefore she doesn't sell directly to consumers. A buyer at Harry & David was able to convince her to make a quantity of 45 units of this exceptional butter. Using a special container that allows Harry &

David to ship the butter directly to customers, the company was able to sell this remarkable find. But Harry & David did more than that. Instead of simply offering the limited-supply butter, Harry & David made it an entire experience by telling customers about the woman who made the butter, including how she came to this calling and how she earns a nice living for her family by making butter for just 10 of the best restaurants in the country; the story was illustrated with pictures that showed where she makes it. The result was curiosity and excitement. For customers who missed out on their opportunity to get the butter, they could still read about the woman's story and request to be put on a list to receive future limited offerings.

These subsets of customers have allowed Harry & David to cultivate the sense of belonging and community, which in turn has unleashed creativity among customers as they share their experiences.

You cannot justify these activities from a profit point of view, but Jim and his team are excited by the ability to deepen relationships with subsets of their community and have some fun with their buyers and their customers, even if the motivation is not financial.

## LIMITED SUPPLY IN ACTION

We've noted quite a few examples in this chapter of the use of limited supply, but let's look at each a little closer so you can understand and apply it in your business.

### INVITATION ONLY

In 2020, Clubhouse took center stage as one of the hottest new social apps. Through this app, people could join rooms in order to listen to or participate in discussions. Many A-list celebrities also joined the app, including Oprah Winfrey, Drake, and Elon Musk. What made this app so popular? The fact that not just anyone could join. In fact, you had to be invited by other Clubhouse members. The catch was that members didn't have unlimited invitations, so they couldn't just invite anyone. While the app had steady growth, an interview between Elon Musk and Robinhood CEO Vlad Tenev on Clubhouse caused demand for invitations to increase. The limitation resulted in invitations being sold on eBay, Craigslist, and Alibaba. Nearly a year after its launch, Clubhouse was valued at $4 billion.[11]

It's not just social platforms that have used the "by invite only" approach and gotten the attention of consumers. Sony had consumers register for a chance to receive an invitation to preorder the PlayStation 5 before the price was even announced; and despite the fact that people didn't know the price, they jumped on the limited opportunity anyway. Amazon has also hosted various products and shopping experiences that were by invitation only, including the Echo Loop, Echo Frames, and Luxury Stores. Even a branding agency took this approach—potential clients had to be invited to talk to the agency. Its website could only be accessed if you were one of the fortunate ones invited.

"By invite only" means that something is limited or exclusive, and based on what we know about scarcity already, it's clear that the value of that invitation will reach golden ticket status as a result. Businesses can use "by invite only" in a variety of ways, such as for access to new or special products, early releases, brand communities, and product wait lists, to name a few.

## JOIN THE EXCLUSIVE GROUP

Similar to limiting the number of invites, businesses can create exclusive groups as a way to use the influential power of limited supply without having a restricted quantity of goods. An exclusive group can come in the form of an event with limited seats available or a network with strict membership criteria. This type of approach appeals to people who want to be unique—to be different from the rest. Take Eliances® as an example.

Eliances.com is a worldwide organization of high-level entrepreneurs and businesspeople that has grown its influence significantly since its inception in 2013. Eliances is the only organization that provides a community "Where Entrepreneurs Align" and hosts many experiences, including weekly "hybrid" (online and in person at the same time) events that connect members with one another in a structured setting where attendees are each given a 60-second window to pitch their Eliances 3G Methodology™ "Got, Give and Get." Every week, the events, which are by invitation only, reach maximum capacity. There is no guarantee that an attendee will receive an invitation to the next event, as the community decides who is accepted back.

It wasn't by accident that the community grew exponentially. David Cogan, the founder of Eliances, explained to me that he carefully studied the model of Ivy League schools, including Harvard, before launching the elite community. He realized that part of the prestige associated with these highly sought-after schools was exclusivity. Not just anyone can get into Harvard, and when you do get the invitation to attend, you better respond quickly.

David took this model and applied it to Eliances. To attend an event, you need to be invited by another member. To become a member, you need to receive an invitation, which is only offered after the feedback from the community and advisory council is gathered and approved. Similar to Harvard, when you do receive the invitation to join, there is a strict deadline to respond. If you miss that deadline, there isn't a second chance to join. According to David, if you have to think about whether to accept the invitation or not, then Eliances is not for you.

David attributes the invitation approach to the culture that has been fostered within the Eliances community. There is a level of excitement at each event, because not only do people want to be there, but they also recognize that they have an exclusive membership and the opportunity to meet billionaires, millionaires, celebrities, entrepreneurs, politicians, athletes, founders, CEOs, influencers, inventors, authors, investors, speakers, and more.

The restriction placed on the attendance of each weekly event has occurred naturally—the room has a maximum capacity. Therefore, physically there are only a limited number of seats available. Additionally, because attendees give a 60-second pitch, only so many people can share during the two-hour meeting. Scarcity occurs naturally. The limited availability is not a gimmick or marketing ploy. According to David, the popularity of the Eliances community has achieved over 500 experiences that reached capacity.

Leading up to the events, invited attendees receive a sequence of emails letting them know the details and how to reserve their seats. Each email subject line indicates that it is a "Private Invite Only" event and includes a prompt to reserve now. As the date approaches, the type of seats available (i.e., online only or in person) is clearly stated. The emails, which are designed to inform invitees of the upcoming gathering, also create a sense of urgency. Because each event is by invite only and quickly runs out of seats, invitees know they have to act fast or they will miss out.

Eliances doesn't use these emails to artificially create a perception of scarcity. Instead, David explains, they use them to educate. In his words, "If you don't educate customers regarding a limitation and then they can't have what you are offering, they will be upset." Eliances' goal, therefore, of notifying invitees that an event is limited is truly to eliminate surprises.

It's not uncommon for members to reserve their seats far in advance of the next event to make sure they don't miss out. It's also not uncommon for the most expensive seats to run out first—those are very limited.

Exclusivity grew the community, but it is sustained by the value that members receive.

## RESTRICTED SUPPLY

Brands know that when there is a restricted supply, the chances of a lot of people having that same item are reduced, and therefore can make the customers able to purchase the scarce product feel special (and agreeable to paying more).

Supreme is a streetwear brand founded in 1994 that sells skateboarding T-shirts, hats, sweatshirts, and other clothing. This company found success by tapping into the idea of supply-related scarcity and relying on the need for uniqueness among its fans. The brand was able to create hype around its label by restricting the amount of clothing products released at a time. Supreme was a big success among teens and young adults who did not want "mainstream" brands.

Some brands purposely limit distribution channels to restrict the availability of their products. For example, Christian Dior sued grocery stores for carrying its products in the nineties because making the Dior products widely available could hurt the company.[12] At the time the case was in court, Peter Norman, who was the managing director of Givenchy, explained how offering high-end fragrances at supermarkets would be problematic: "Shopping for perfumes should be a pleasant and aspirational experience. By placing our products among vegetables and slashing the prices, their desirability is undermined."[13] A shopping cart with a mix of eggs, milk, vegetables, and Christian Dior fragrance just doesn't scream exclusive. Luxury brands have continued to fight to control availability.

For some businesses, it will make sense to follow the examples of these brands that are purposely restricting supply. That could mean only producing a small quantity at a time, such as in the Supreme example, or limiting the distribution channels, such as in the case of Christian Dior. It could also mean a strong focus on direct-to-consumer sales, which will create an environment in which the supply and distribution channels can be restricted.

## THE FIGHT TO CONTROL AVAILABILITY ONLINE

Any company striving for the impression of exclusivity or rarity combats available supply in a different way than companies did in the past, thanks to the internet.

The online market allows us to get anything we want at any time we want. This wide access has also increased transactions with the gray market, which involves unauthorized resellers and unofficial channels within the supply chain. To combat the wide spread of gray market transactions, which can damage the air of exclusivity among brands, many companies have focused more efforts on boosting their direct-to-consumer sales. For example, KitchenAid, Urban Decay, and MAC have all devoted significant efforts to website sales to increase direct-to-consumer transactions and ensure their customers are receiving the products they want directly from the company.

Dyson Corporation is another good example. The company focuses on controlling distribution and attracting customers to purchase directly from the Dyson website through price matching, product financing, and other attractive options.[14]

Companies are also investing in and using modern technology such as artificial intelligence and automation to identify unauthorized sellers and channels. These types of technologies can detect inconsistencies in product images, descriptions, and promotions.[15] By controlling the distribution channels, companies can control the availability and also the perceived scarcity, or exclusivity, of their products.

---

Restricted supply can apply to services, too. A friend of mine, Grace, provides a great example of how limiting the number of clients became an effective business model.

Grace spent years working in the digital marketing industry at various agencies. When she decided to step out on her own and start her own social media marketing business, she was worried about how she would get new clients. She had no desire to create a large business, but instead wanted to remain a solopreneur with only a handful of clients.

Grace spent weeks networking within her local business community and started to pick up clients here and there and was also getting good results for each of them. Eventually, word spread about her work, and she started to get more referrals.

Then something happened that significantly increased demand for Grace's services.

During a call with a potential lead who was referred to Grace, she shared that because she's a consultant and doesn't work at a big company, she could only work with a small number of clients at a time. Grace unknowingly and unintentionally used restricted supply to her advantage—not with a product, but with her time.

Without meaning to, Grace had communicated scarcity and accidently stumbled on a tactic that would help her close deals on projects she *wanted* to work on.

Grace's example is a great one for business owners, consultants, and/or salespeople within a service business. Time is naturally limited in service-oriented businesses, and communicating the current availability or criteria to become a customer or client can go a long way in increasing sales.

## SHORT RENEWAL CYCLE

Some companies have taken to limiting supply through short renewal cycles. These businesses create smaller collections more frequently and shorten product life cycles. This approach allows these businesses to address the need for uniqueness among customers. Perhaps one of the best examples of a company utilizing a short renewal cycle is the fast fashion company Zara.

Instead of following the typical two-season model common among fashion retailers, Zara creates as many as 20 fashion seasons per year. Zara replenishes products quickly based on customer demand. Unlike other brands that take an average of six months to produce new items and deliver them to stores, Zara is able to cut this time to less than three weeks. In a normal season, Zara can produce around 11,000 different items, compared with competitors that can only produce 2,000 to 4,000. However, even more interesting and relevant to the discussion of scarcity is that Zara also regularly rotates the assortment of products in stores.[16] When product availability is the norm for most retailers, Zara's approach is the opposite—purposely limit product availability through short renewal cycles and limited supply.[17] Additionally, if a product is out of a particular size, it is company policy to remove that product from the sales floor and place it in the backroom until all sizes are available. Because of the quick product cycle, sizes often run out fast. If production has stopped for that product, it will remain in the backroom to be placed on clearance later; or if it is a popular item, it will be moved to a warehouse and sent to stores with the highest sales for that item.[18]

This short renewal cycle, moving of products to the backroom and quick product turnover due to limited supply creates a perception of scarcity in the consumer's mind. Zara's target customers are young people who want to buy fashionable and trendy clothes at an inexpensive price. These customers visit the stores frequently because they know the selection will change. They also know that if they see something they like, they better buy it because it might not be there next time. The other interesting aspect of this approach is that it satisfies the need for uniqueness. Thus, the concern of being like everyone else, by wearing a popular clothing item, diminishes because there is such a limited supply of products.

This strategy works for companies not in the fast fashion industry, as well. Grocery stores can limit availability of special collections of products or brands. Businesses can create pop-up stores, which creates the mentality of what is here today will be gone tomorrow. Even vendors at local farmers' markets can reap the benefits of this mentality, because by their very nature, products are limited and not always available for purchase.[19]

## EXCLUSIVE EXPERIENCE

Exclusive experiences are another effective form of supply-related scarcity, and this approach is one of the easiest for businesses to implement. Take my local aquarium as an example.

The aquarium is the largest in Arizona (it holds more than 2 million gallons of water . . . in the middle of the desert!).[20] Back when my son was in elementary school, he developed a deep interest in penguins. So much so, that his room was decorated in penguins, he had penguin stuffed animals, a penguin lunchbox, penguin T-shirts, and so on. You get the idea.

Around this same time, his school went on a field trip to the aquarium, and I volunteered to be a parent chaperone. While we were walking through the building and admiring the many marine animals, we saw a sign promoting the Penguin Encounter, where you could play with penguins. For 45 minutes, you could get an "up close and personal meeting with an African Penguin."[21] As soon as we got home, I went on the aquarium's website to reserve our spot. The encounter price would be in addition to the general admission ticket—making this a pretty costly event. I started to waver a bit on my decision to order our tickets, but how could we pass on this exclusive opportunity when my son loved penguins so much?

The website played into this by making it obvious that this event was special and limited. It was clearly stated that each session was limited to a certain number of participants. There was also a prompt to reserve now to get your spot. Clicking the "Book Now" button only confirmed this exclusivity, as we had to book far in advance because the earlier spots were all taken.

Was it worth it? Yes. My son showed up for his encounter with the penguins dressed as a penguin. I don't think it gets any more special than that.

This aquarium example is just one instance of a business creating an exclusive experience. When M&M'S was deciding on a new crunchy flavor, the company created an immersive pop-up in New York City. The pop-up gave customers the opportunity to interact with the proposed crunchy flavors of raspberry, espresso, and mint.[22] The M&M'S experience included "flavor rooms," which had their own fragrances and decor based on a certain flavor. There were snack and drink lounges that even featured M&M-themed cocktails.[23] Why would the brand go to such lengths to select a new flavor? According to Tanya Berman, the VP of Chocolate at Mars at the time of the pop-up, "The event itself is because our fans at M&M's love to be part of how we create a flavor. We get ideas all the time from them, whether it's on social [or] online; people even write to us because they love the variety and the flavor." And fans got their say by selecting mint as the new flavor.[24]

No matter the industry, any business can create an exclusive experience and, as M&M'S so creatively did, give customers a chance to interact with the brand.

## VIP STATUS

By its very construct, the designation "VIP" (very important person) creates a special membership. In a way, First Lady Mary Todd Lincoln created VIP status among Washington society in 1862.[25] By allowing only a select group of people to attend an evening ball at the White House, the event became that much more alluring.

VIP memberships and groups fall into the category of supply-related scarcity. Only a certain number of these types of memberships are provided, and many are based on either being a top customer or being willing to pay a premium. The travel, hospitality, and entertainment industries all have these types of memberships. Consider Marriott Bonvoy™ Lifetime Elite status. Once you stay a certain number of nights at a Marriott hotel, you receive special perks such as late checkouts and room upgrades. The more you stay and spend, the higher your status.

Being a VIP member makes us feel that we are part of a prestigious group, and we begin to differentiate ourselves from those with less status. Because these memberships are designed to appear elite or even rare, the perception of scarcity prevails and the membership becomes desirable. Offering VIP memberships or status levels is profitable for businesses because consumers are willing to spend the extra money for the better designation.[26] This is despite the fact that many VIP members do not receive significantly different services than non-VIP members. What they are paying for is the exclusivity.

———

Limited edition is also a form of supply-related scarcity, and because it is so prevalent and effective, the entire next chapter is dedicated to this form of supply-related scarcity.

## KEY SELLING POINTS

- Something that has a limited or restricted supply is appealing to people who are looking for prestige, respect, or uniqueness.

- Limited or restricted supply can also come in the form of invitations, privileges, events, or services, and suggests that fewer people will have access.

- Messages must be made in a way that suggests there is a limited supply versus low quantity due to popular demand.

# CHAPTER 8

# "Only While Supplies Last!"

HOW MUCH WOULD YOU pay for a good night's sleep? For some people, the answer is $175,000. In 2013, British mattress manufacturer Savoir Beds launched a limited-edition "Royal Bed" with a hefty price tag of $175,000.[1] Each mattress required more than 700 hours of labor to produce. At that price, you might be wondering if the mattress was made of gold. While the mattress might not have been filled with gold flakes, it did contain bundles of curled Latin American horsetail hair (used to absorb moisture, regulate body temperature, and provide natural spring), masses of pure Mongolian cashmere, and plenty of specially woven silk (if strung, the silk strand would be nearly 1,600 miles long).[2] To craft such a mattress, artisans spread out the cashmere and horse hair and then combed through it to calculate how much was required for an individual bed. Only 60 Royal Bed mattresses were produced.

Savoir's managing director at the time, Alistair Hughes, admitted that the mattress wasn't for everyone. How could it be at that price? "No one can deny that it's a lot of money, but for the kind of people who spend $10,000 a night staying in presidential suites or driving a fabulous car, it's something that could very well appeal," read Hughes's quote in *Time* magazine.

The Royal Bed was undoubtedly an elite product that only a few could afford. It was also the classic example of a limited-edition product. Scarce products are almost always considered to be of better quality and/or value, as we have seen in previous chapters. Limited edition is a type of supply-related scarcity (as we just learned about in Chapter 7), but because it's so prevalent and effective, the topic deserves its own chapter.

Limited-edition scarcity involves deliberately limiting the supply of a product and catering to the desire for exclusivity. Unlike demand-related scarcity, meaning the products are scarce because of popularity, limited-edition scarcity is based on the limited number of units produced and is typically a slightly modified version of the regular product.

Remember Starbucks's Unicorn Frappuccino? Not only was the drink offered for a limited time; it was also a limited-edition item. The drink consisted of blended crème, pink powder, mango syrup, and sour blue drizzle—and of course, topped off with vanilla whipped cream. "Like its mythical namesake, the Unicorn Frappuccino blended crème comes with a bit of magic, starting as a purple beverage with swirls of blue and a first taste that is sweet and fruity, but give it a stir and its color changes to pink, and the flavor evolves to tangy and tart. The more swirl, the more the beverage's color and flavors transform," Starbucks explained in a statement.[3] Who *wouldn't* want a "bit of magic"?

The drink was released during the unicorn trend of 2017 when unicorns made a comeback and turned into the latest fad. From April 19, 2017, to April 23, 2017, the drinks were available at participating locations, but only while supplies lasted. The result was a frenzy of consumers flocking to Starbucks nationwide to get their own elusive unicorn drink. A *USA Today* headline read, "People Are Freaking Out over Starbucks Unicorn Frappuccino." And freaking out they were. Social media feeds were full of pictures of the Unicorn Frappuccino.

I still remember the week the drink was released. I was teaching a marketing course at the university, and before class began, a student asked if I had tried the Unicorn Frappuccino. I believe my response was something to the effect of, "The what Frappuccino?" Immediately two other students joined the conversation and animatedly described the drink. One student took out her phone and opened Instagram to show me pictures that were in her feed of friends who tried the drink. The images showed a colorful drink in a variety of backgrounds. It turns out that during the promotion of the sugary drink, there were close to 155,000 posts on Instagram, which drove a significant amount of people to their local Starbucks before it sold out.[4] The drink had a bigger impact, though, on Starbucks's bottom line. When compared with the previous period, the total dollar amount of sales increased in stores.[5]

Limited-edition products, such as the Royal Mattress and Unicorn Frappuccino, build upon the belief that scarce items can be used to differentiate ourselves from others. By their very nature, limited-edition products are scarce because both the quantity of the product and the time available are, well, limited. Limited-edition products are attractive to people who desire to be unique and see the products as a form of self-expression. As

Savoir's managing director was quick to explain, the Royal Bed wasn't for everyone; it was only for a select group of people who have the means and desire to invest in the six-figure mattress.

There are many forms of limited-edition scarcity, ranging from special packaging, unique design, line extension, special collections, all the way to product bundles. (The Unicorn Frappuccino is an example of a line extension.)

Korbel Champagne Cellars provides a good example of product packaging. In 2015, Korbel Champagne Cellars released a limited-edition Korbel Brut Rosé bottle to celebrate Valentine's Day. The ingredients of the Brut Rosé did not change; only the outside of the bottle got an update. The label was decorated with red lip prints, and foil that looked like black lace wrapped the top of the bottle.[6] It was a success and caused Korbel to continue to release new limited editions for Valentine's Day, including the "Love Letter" edition that featured a design of pink lettering meant to depict handwritten love notes.

There are also many examples of brands using unique designs to develop limited-edition versions, including Yamaha (limited-edition pianos), BMW (special-edition model of the 7 series to celebrate 40 years of the series), and Coca-Cola's holiday-edition packaging. Luxury goods especially tend to benefit from a unique design, as in the case of Panerai.

## WATCHES, THE ITALIAN NAVY, AND SYLVESTER STALLONE

In 1860, Giovanni Panerai opened his first watchmaker's shop on Ponte alle Grazie in Florence, but it wasn't until more than 100 years later that the Italian watch company experienced the power of scarcity firsthand.

While the original workshop was a small family-owned business specializing in high-quality pocket watches, the business expanded and eventually began producing high-precision instruments for the Italian Royal Navy.[7] The company began experimenting with a radium-based powder that would cause its watches to glow in the dark, a feature that was incredibly helpful to Italian navy divers. The mixture was named Radiomir, which was included in a patent awarded to Panerai. Radiomir was also the name given to Panerai's first model of wristwatch.

For years, Panerai created new innovations for watches, ranging from titanium cases to rugged straps to another radiant substance that was branded Luminor.[8] In 1993, Panerai decided to step into the consumer watch market by launching three collections, which included numbered and limited editions (the 44-mm Luminor, Luminor Marina, and the 42-mm Mare Nostrum chronograph, to be specific). These special editions were inspired by the historical watch models created for the underwater division of the Italian navy. The collection was unveiled on September 10, 1993, in the Military Harbor of La Spezia, on the Italian navy cruiser *Durand de la Penne.*[9] The ceremony was attended by the supreme head of the Italian diving department at the time. Two years later, Sylvester Stallone wore a Panerai watch in the movie *Daylight,* and demand grew quickly among consumers. In 1997, Vendome Group bought Panerai and grew it into a global brand.[10]

Since the 1993 launch into the consumer market, Panerai has continued with the strategy of producing limited editions. There are basic models available, which don't change. However, every year, new versions are introduced with new features. Historical models that have been off the market for decades are occasionally updated and released. The products are released in limited quantities anywhere from 250 to 2,000 at a time, depending on the model.[11] The company takes an extra step with the limited edition that only fuels the demand and anticipation—it unveils the new models far in advance of their release. Panerai will typically reveal the models in the beginning of the year with release later in the year. As the anticipation grows, it is not uncommon for Panerai fans to buy as quickly as they can once the models are released because of the fear of missing out. This demand has continued for over 20 years.

Collectors and Panerai enthusiasts even have a place to gather and share their collections: Paneristi.com. The website, started in 2000, facilitates discussions around Panerai products, including a forum titled, "What are you wearing today?" There is also a private Facebook group devoted to fans with over 23,000 members (as of August 2021). The community has grown organically with people who are passionate about the brand.

In 2010, Panerai did something that solidified the community's love of the brand. Panerai asked the community for input on what the perfect Panerai model would look like. The PAM 360 model was therefore born as a tribute to the community on the website's tenth anniversary. To make it even more meaningful, the watch was inscribed on the back with "paneristi.com" and "Tenth Anniversary." There were only 300 units of this model available.

This special watch was not sold in stores. Instead, it was available for purchase through a lottery among the members of the Paneristi community only.[12] Over 2,600 Paneristi members scrambled to get their PAM 360 model, but the $7,000 watches were sold out almost instantly.[13]

Not only did Panerai develop and continue to follow a strategy of limited-edition products, but the company also recognized its customers and actively engaged with them to make them feel like they were truly part of the brand.

# I WANT TO EXPRESS MYSELF

Self-expression: "The expression of one's own personality;
assertion of one's individual traits."

MERRIAM-WEBSTER[14]

Social media provides a significant platform for self-expression. It provides an outlet to share who we are and what we believe. Some of this comes from the words we share, but a lot comes from the images we post. Social media in particular fosters the "trading-up" phenomenon, which is our tendency to attain achievement by consuming products that make us feel like a better version of ourselves. Were you able to buy a bottle of the 2020 Yellowstone Limited Edition Bourbon? Did you get a pair of Nike Dunk Low SE shoes before they sold out? If so, this might not have been news you kept to yourself. Instead, you told people and posted pictures on social media of you enjoying these hard-to-get products.

Consumers today often treat social media as a reference group, meaning they compare themselves to others within their social networks and often turn to them when making decisions. On the same note, they make purchases for the purpose of recognition in these reference groups.[15] With the prevalence of social media, such as Instagram and Facebook, scarce products are often used as a form of self-expression. These rare items lead to differentiation and uniqueness.

In the past, limited-edition products were mainly focused on enthusiasts, such as car lovers or art collectors. But thanks to social media, the demand for self-expression has grown, and limited-edition items are becoming even more desirable. Today we can express ourselves through products rather than other forms of social recognition, and from a business perspective, customers will have a higher intention to purchase products if those products provide a high level of self-expression.

## CONSUMING THE CONSPICUOUS

**Why fit in when you were born to stand out?**
DR. SUESS[16]

Limited edition shines the brightest among conspicuous consumption goods (remember those are items such as automobiles, jewelry, clothing . . . anything that is prominently visible to other people). When we strive for conspicuousness, we are proud to be seen, whether that is with our hard-to-find bourbon bottle or new designer glasses. Buying products that are conspicuous can satisfy our desire to stand out from others.[17] At the same time, we are often drawn to limited-edition products from an emotional appeal. These types of products make us feel worthy and boost our perceived value of ourselves. Now this might not happen if you purchase a can of Coca-Cola with a picture of Santa Claus (i.e., the Christmas limited edition), but you might get that sense of worthiness and value from, say, a Panerai special-edition wristwatch. When a product is used as a status symbol, it can also give the perception of a high social status. This leads to not only the feeling of being worthy, but also the perception of being envied and respected.[18]

"Conspicuous consumption of valuable goods is a means of reputability to the gentleman of leisure," explained Thorstein Veblen in 1899 in his famous book, *The Theory of the Leisure Class*.[19] The gentlemen of leisure referred to by Veblen are considered the elite members of society. The theory of the leisure class argues that these elite members pursue self-respect from their peers through the possession, or display, of wealth.[20] According to Veblen, wealth and power can be implied through publicly visible goods and services. Through this signaling of wealth and power, you could achieve social status, per Veblen.

Veblen's original concept of conspicuous consumption was later expanded by other theorists, who argued that products can satisfy a range of social needs, including the need to be respected, admired, and envied. Conspicuous consumption has even been tied to the need to gain leadership.[21] Let's take a closer look into how this works.

If you have the social need to be admired, owning a product that everyone else has (i.e., it's popular) doesn't satisfy that need. Instead, owning a product that is limited in supply, such as a limited-edition product, does. Now you own something that not a lot of other people have.

Veblen's theory has been coined the "Veblen effect" and is defined as "a willingness to pay a higher price for a functionally equivalent good."[22] For example, based on the Veblen effect, the higher that you price the item, the more that people will buy it. This aligns with what is known already about limited-edition items. Limited-edition scarcity is typically associated with high price levels, and the sales of such products can actually decrease at low price points.[23]

One marketing manager of luxury goods explained that "our customers do not want to pay less. If we halved the price of all our products, we would double our sales for six months and then we would sell nothing."[24] The *Economist* also warned about the Veblen effect in that retailers could harm their products' images by selling them too cheaply. The Veblen effect when coupled with limited-edition scarcity can significantly increase sales.

## TYPES OF LIMITED EDITION

Brands often create line extensions or vary the features of products to make them limited. Take BMW as an example (we briefly touched on this earlier). To celebrate the 40-year anniversary of the 7 series, in 2017 BMW introduced a limited-edition model with special color and design features. The catch? The model was only available at the BMW Dingolfing plant in Germany, a geographical limit known as a "territorial limitation."[25]

As we have discussed, we know that limited editions appeal to people who want to stand out and, in some cases, show social status. But there are many ways in which companies can use a limited-edition strategy that addresses this group as well as many others, including events, service bundles, twists, packaging, and collaborations. Let's dive into some of them, including how other companies have put them into practice.

### EVENTS FOR THE ENTHUSIASTS

When you combine a limited-edition product with an event with limited tickets, the result is a frenzy of buyers.

*A case in point:* It was a cold, dreary day in the middle of winter in Schaumburg, Illinois, a Chicago suburb. That didn't deter people from all over the country from traveling to Schaumburg, where they packed into a RAM Restaurant and Brewery, a chain brewery. They were there for Chaos Day.[26] Some enthusiasts drove as far as 1,200 miles to get to the exclusive event with the intent to purchase the brewery's limited-edition beer.

The event was first held in 2016 with the purpose of celebrating the release of Chaos, RAM's barrel-aged stout. Within two months of the tickets for Chaos Day going on sale, they sold out. That is not too bad for a brand-new event. But what happened the next year showed scarcity in action. When the $74.99 tickets for the 2017 event went on sale, 400 sold in less than a minute, causing the event to sell out immediately.[27]

RAM's limited-edition stout was one of the most pursued beers among traders throughout the country. Limited-production brews, such as RAM's 800-bottle supply, have been known to go on illegal secondary markets for hundreds of dollars each. But one of the biggest draws for beer aficionados is the bragging rights. They find out about these hard-to-come-by brews on beer forums, on ratings sites, and from friends in the craft beer community.

Although the beer market is highly competitive, scarcity helped this brewpub chain stand out from the competition. Holding an event to showcase the limited-edition brew only catapulted the beer hunter's desire to get that rare bottle of beer. Of course, the beer was good, too.

As well, many wineries host events for members when releasing the season's special-edition varietals. But it's a strategy that is not just limited to the liquor industry. Any business with a limited-edition product or service can use this technique. A retailer might host an "after-hours" party for certain customers to shop the newest, limited-edition product lines. A gym might hold an open house for potential customers and offer limited-edition services or pricing packages. A software provider might put on a one-day conference to announce a new limited-edition suite. The goal is to identify the type of event that best aligns with the limited-edition item and the target customers.

## SERVICE BUNDLES

Many service-oriented businesses have used limited edition to their advantage, in the form of service bundles. These bundles might include special pricing for insurance or cable service. Even salons and med spas use bundles that offer price discounts but are still considered limited edition.

## A SLIGHT TWIST ON THE ORIGINAL

A limited-edition item is most often a slight twist on the original. As noted earlier, Yamaha is known for creating limited-edition piano models and limiting supply. In 2016, the company introduced the Butterfly Limited Edition Model, which was part of a series of special-edition marquetry pianos from Bösendorfer, the premier manufacturer of handcrafted and special-design instruments. The piano had a floral and butterfly motif with a unique cabinet design instead of the usual polished ebony or wood finish. Only nine pianos were available, and they were sold to stores worldwide. As you can imagine, the pianos sold out quickly.

Oreos has sold countless crunchy cookies by putting a spin on the classic snack. There is a small team dedicated to creating special-edition Oreos, and it is one busy team. Since 2012, there have been 65 different special flavors, including Birthday Cake Oreos, Jelly Donut Oreos, Banana Split Oreos, Blueberry Pie Oreos, Key Lime Pie Oreos, and Root Beer Float Oreos, and let's not forget Chicken Wing Oreos and Wasabi Oreos.[28] New flavor ideas are developed 18 to 24 months before being released. The team begins with 50 new flavor concepts and then whittles the list down to around a dozen. The team will even work with chefs to determine what is trending.[29] Think about that process next time you are at the store and walk by the display of salmon-colored Oreos with malachite-green filling (in celebration of Lady Gaga and her album *Chromatica*). Instead of producing a completely new product, a business can make a simple modification, such as a different flavor (e.g., Oreos), scent, color, or material than the original. Even the design can be changed to make a product a limited-edition item, which is what Yamaha did with its piano.

## PACKAGING

Nonluxury items, such as everyday items you would pick up from the grocery store, see an uptick in sales with a change in product packaging. It's one of the reasons companies routinely change their product packaging. There is actually a name for it: "limited-edition packaging." It is considered a scarcity tactic by all means because there is a restriction of some sort, making it not always available. With limited-edition packaging, the package itself creates the limited offer. There tends to be labeling that states something to the effect of "limited edition" or "special edition."

For many businesses, limited-edition packaging is an effective way to reap the benefits of the scarcity principle without having to reformat the actual product itself. The examples of limited-edition packaging are endless and provide inspiration. Absolut Vodka created the end-of-the-year Bling-Bling limited bottle in 2006 and also the Absolut London bottle that celebrated the United Kingdom capital (only 518,000 bottles were released). Bottle Green, which produces sparkling water, created limited-edition bottles supporting a breast cancer charity. Makeup company Urban Decay released a limited-edition makeup palette based on the *Game of Thrones*. The eyeshadow palette had a pop-up iron throne and brushes that resembled swords from the popular show. Even Dole bananas, which only has a sticker to work with, jumped into the limited-edition packaging arena. The company created the campaign "Powering the Hero Within" that was aimed at recognizing women who use their powers. The stickers included Captain Marvel female characters.[30] The appeal for companies to embrace limited-edition packaging is that it creates the same perception of scarcity without having to re-create the product or produce a limited line extension.

## COLLABORATIONS

Collaborations with celebrities to create limited-edition items has led to skyrocketing sales for many companies, and there are countless examples: Nike and Michael Jordan (Air Jordans), Reese Witherspoon and Crate and Barrel, Demi Lovato and Fabletics, and Miley Cyrus and Converse. However, collaborating with a widely known celebrity might not be possible for every business. In the age of influencers, a "celebrity" doesn't have to be an A-list actor or actress or even a professional athlete. A celebrity could be an influencer who has an audience base that aligns with the customers a business is trying to target. A specific line of products or services can be renamed, repackaged, or modified for the influencer's fans.

Brands can also collaborate to create limited-edition products or services. How might this work? A business can partner with another to provide a streamlined service to customers, such as an accounting software provider and payroll servicer offering a limited-edition service bundle. Businesses can combine strengths to create a unique product, such as an artist and jeweler working together to develop a limited-edition line of jewelry. What makes this strategy so effective is that now the brands have double their audience or customer base.

Two Norwegian companies, fashion brand HAiK and eyewear company Kaibosh, joined forces to create limited-edition reversible sunglasses that gave the option of two different frames. The promotional video took a humorous approach to the special sunglasses by featuring a female customer who explained how hard it is for her to make decisions. The sunglasses solved the problem for her.

The Two Way sunglasses featured a special hinge that allowed the arms (aka temples) to flip to the other side of the frame. The limited-edition sunglasses were only available online and in select stores. The attraction of these types of collaborations is not only the special-edition aspect, but also the uncertainty whether the brands will ever collaborate again. This concept applies to any size business.

Sometimes there is even a frenzy over products featuring a limited-time collaboration, as in the example of FENDI x SKIMS, showing the scarcity principle in action.

## YOU CAN'T PAY TO GET YOUR WAY IN

Kim Kardashian's SKIMS brand collaborated with Fendi to create an exclusive line of high-end fashion. News of the collection caused a flurry of excitement.

A video posted on TMZ.com showed a long line of shoppers anxiously awaiting their turn to enter the Beverly Hills Fendi store and purchase from the limited-edition FENDI x SKIMS collection. Emotions quickly became heated as one woman was accused of paying her way to cut in line. The shoppers shouted accusations about the alleged line cutter: "She cut the line!" "She paid her to let her in!" "No cuts, sis!"

Online shoppers were just as determined. Within one minute of launching the FENDI x SKIMS collection online, sales reached $1 million. Everything within the limited-edition line was reportedly quickly sold out. There was no doubt there would be competition to buy a product from this limited collection. In fact, over 300,000 people signed up to be on the wait list prior to the collection's launch.

Even high-end limited-edition products can cause a physiological reaction and create a strong sense of competition.

## LIMITED-EDITION PRODUCTS TIED TO POPULAR EVENTS

Limited-edition products that are tied to a popular event (an event not connected with the company) are another great example and can create brand affinity. Dean Barrett, retired McDonald's Senior Vice President of Global Marketing, shared how McDonald's has found success with promoting limited-edition products. Think about the Happy Meal. Happy Meals are tied with some of the largest properties in the world and give McDonald's customers a way to interact with movies or properties as they are released in the marketplace. A tie-in drives sales of Happy Meals, but also brand affinity because McDonald's is associated with the popular movie or entity at the time.

Similar to what McDonald's does, a business can develop a special product, service, or packaging associated with a popular event. Of course, don't forget there are licensing and trademark considerations, so extra steps might be needed if exploring this option.

While we know that limited-edition and supply-related scarcity can do wonders for businesses, scarcity caused by popularity can also be effective. The next chapter talks about the customers this type of scarcity appeals to and how businesses can use it.

## KEY SELLING POINTS

- Limited-edition products build upon the belief that scarce items can be used to differentiate ourselves from others.

- Limited-edition products are attractive to people who desire to be unique and see the products as a form of self-expression.

- Limited edition shines the brightest among conspicuous consumption goods.

- We are often drawn to limited-edition products from an emotional appeal. These types of products make us feel worthy and boost our perceived value of ourselves.

- There are many ways in which companies can use a limited-edition strategy including events, service bundles, twists, packaging, and collaborations.

# CHAPTER 9

# Exclusive or Popular?

SIX-YEAR-OLD LUKE LOOKED UP at his mom (and my friend), Emily, with his big blue eyes. He moved the wisp of hair that had fallen over his cheek and took a deep breath. What he was about to ask his mom was something he had been practicing all morning. He wanted to get his question just right. Finally, he exhaled and made his request: could they get a dog? The family had never owned a dog, and it was something that Luke had wanted his entire life (his words). Just in case his mom said no, he already had a backup plan. He would ask Santa.

Emily's heart melted, and truth be told, she had already been talking to her husband, Shane, about getting a dog. After a lot of back-and-forth discussion, they made the decision to get Luke a labradoodle. With so many horror stories of puppy mills and unscrupulous "puppy sellers," Emily wanted to get a labradoodle from a breeder who was well known and trusted. She called her friend who had purchased a labradoodle the year prior and was given the breeder's contact information. Emily called the breeder, Jane, and was told that a litter of puppies would be born within the next two weeks. However, given that labradoodles were in high demand and Jane was picky about whom she would let take one of her puppies home, she explained to Emily that she would need to keep an eye on Jane's Facebook page to find out when the litter was born. Then, and only then, would Jane accept applications to buy one of her puppies. She also explained to Emily that she time-stamps the applications, so the sooner she applied, the better her odds.

From that moment on, Emily checked the Facebook page religiously throughout the day. It became an obsession, and she wanted to make sure she was one of the first to apply. A week had passed, and Emily and her kids were on the way home from the zoo. It had been two hours since she last checked the Facebook page, and she was starting to feel anxious. What if the puppies had been born while they were at the zoo and she missed her chance to submit an application? As soon as they pulled in the driveway and Emily parked the car, she opened her Facebook app on her phone. Lo and behold, the puppies *had* been born while she was at the zoo. Emily's heart began to race. She sent the kids in the house, while she sat in the car and filled out the application as fast as she could. Within an hour of the puppies' birth, Emily had managed to get in her application. Apparently, though, she wasn't the only one who had been keeping a close eye on the Facebook page anxiously awaiting the puppies' arrival. Just three hours after their birth, the breeder posted a message on Facebook that she was no longer accepting applications because of the sheer volume she had already received.

Emily and her family were officially put on the list for the new litter. Twelve weeks later, Luke had his new little puppy, Charlie.

What happened here was exclusivity (you had to apply to get a puppy) and high demand. Let's get more into the latter.

————————

Previously we looked at what scarcity does to the perceived value of an item. In general, the harder something is to get, the more we want it—and this spills over into how we view the value of the item. Yet when an item is scarce because of high demand versus other circumstances like limited supply or time, the perceived value is *even stronger*. This increased desire for the scarce product is at least partially based on what we believe is the underlying reason for the shortage.[1]

This type of scarcity (the kind that's due to high demand or popularity) has a different impact than the other forms of scarcity, especially scarcity caused by a time restriction (see Chapter 6) or limited supply (see Chapter 7). This form of scarcity creates a feeling of urgency, based on the belief that once a product is sold out, the chance to own that product is gone forever. Demand-related scarcity can occur when businesses produce inadequate product quantities to meet demand, as well as when businesses distribute a competitive number of products to retail stores.

This situation has been witnessed when retailers advertise a certain available quantity of a product in each store or on websites when the remaining product quantity is shown on the product page. In these scenarios, marketers will include such messages as "in popular demand" or "nearly sold out due to high demand." When we are exposed to these messages, we begin to feel as though we are in competition with others to possess the products. Therefore, when something is popular and the quantities are limited, it ignites the spirit of competition within us, more so than when scarcity is caused by a time restriction.[2] Numerous studies on scarcity have supported the idea that demand-related scarcity has a great effect on us because of the competitive environment it creates. Etsy is great at creating this sense of competition. Not only will you be made aware if the quantity of the item is low, such as there is only one left; you will also be notified how many people have the item in their shopping carts. Now the first one to the order finish line wins!

The concept that scarcity threatens our freedom is especially prevalent with demand-related scarcity.[3] We want our freedom and independence to purchase anything we want whenever we want. Therefore, scarcity due to high demand propels us to do something immediately.

A new luxury condominium complex in Scottsdale (Arizona) used popular demand to push the sales of its units. A prominent sign outside the high-end complex stated in bold red type, "Over 90% Sold." A one-bedroom condo was priced at $600,000 while a three-bedroom condo was priced at $1 million These were prices that fell within the top 5 percent tier of condos in the area. What made this approach successful was not just that scarcity was used for this high-involvement product, but that the company regularly updated the sign outside the building. Prior to saying that 90 percent had been sold, the sign stated 80 percent sold. Showing people that their chance to own was running out—getting scarcer—helped drive sales.

There is even more to demand-related scarcity. An Australian professor, Dr. Rajat Roy, conducted two experiments that analyzed envy and how it relates to limited supply and demand-related scarcity.[4] Based on his findings, Dr. Roy concluded that when we experience envy as consumers, we perceive a product to have a higher value and our intention to purchase that item increases, but more so with demand-related scarcity appeals than supply-related scarcity appeals.

## LIMITED SUPPLY VERSUS POPULARITY

While supply-related scarcity (i.e., limited supply, limited edition) might seem very similar to demand-related scarcity, there are some key differences. Supply-related scarcity appeals have been known to create a sense of exclusivity. Demand-related scarcity appeals indicate competition and social acceptance, as well as product value.[5] For example, when we identify that a product is scarce, we logically assume that the scarcity is the result of other consumers buying the product in large quantities because the product is good.[6] When quantities are low because of high demand, we also desire the product because owning the item would create a sense of "winning" the competition.

Our past experiences with demand-related scarcity can also influence our purchases. For example, my friend Michelle recalls a time when she purchased tickets to a seasonal event because she remembered it sold out the year before. The event was a haunted corn maze that ran from mid-September to the end of October in connection with Halloween. When Michelle had tried to purchase tickets one October, the maze was already sold out for every night. She described her frustration with not being able to take her husband and teenage boys and decided that it wouldn't happen again the next year. Michelle signed up for the maze's email list so that she could be on top of her purchase the following October. Sure enough, as September rolled around, emails from the maze started going out notifying subscribers about ticket availability. Within two weeks, an email was sent that indicated tickets were nearly sold out. Because Michelle had experienced the sellout before, she immediately purchased her tickets upon seeing that email. The high demand had spurred her purchase, but the updates about availability sent out from the company were what closed the deal.

Most of us are susceptible to demand-related scarcity, depending on the situation. However, this type of scarcity tends to have a greater effect on people with a high need for conformity.

## DON'T STRAY FROM THE HERD

Scarcity that is caused by demand entices people who want to feel included and/or identify with a certain group. We talked about need for uniqueness, but there is an opposing need that exists in many of us, too: the need for conformity. Because we are inherently social beings, we desire to be part of a cohort. It's part of our biological makeup. That means we might look to others within a group—whether a large group (e.g., people our age or in our social class) or small group (e.g., people who share our interests, such as art lovers, food connoisseurs, etc.)—to determine the norms and rules. This includes what we think, what we believe, how we behave, and even what we buy. When we have a high need for conformity, we will value a product by the number of people buying it. We choose the scarce product *because* other people are buying it.

Using wine as the subject, one study tested whether empty shelf space would influence a shopper's choice.[7] Given two options, wine from a fully stocked shelf and wine from a nearly empty shelf, people overwhelmingly selected the one from the empty shelf. The shoppers assumed that if the wine was scarce, it must be popular—and if it was popular, it must be good.

Conformity to a social group might be indicated by owning a scarce product that the group values. Take sneakerheads as an example. Sneakerheads are people who collect and trade sneakers as a hobby. They look for sneakers that are in high demand and selling out. Often they resell them for double or even quadruple what they paid. The people who buy the sneakers from sneakerheads are willing to pay a premium because they know the shoes are sold out and they fear a lost opportunity.

## EVERYBODY'S DOING IT

We know that scarcity can lead to a perception of value, but this notion is even more pronounced when the item is scarce because of high demand.[8] This is consistent with the bandwagon effect, which asserts that we prefer popular products because popularity insinuates the quality of the product. The bandwagon effect refers to the level at which the demand for a product is increased because others are also consuming the same product.[9]

The underlying concept of the bandwagon effect is the existence of a relationship between our increased preference for a product and the number of other people buying that product.[10] The idea is that popular products are desirable and must be of high quality, thus prompting us to join the bandwagon. This effect can be seen in various market sectors and industries, such as the restaurant industry, and numerous events. To put it simply, when a significant number of people want a product, it makes us want the product as well. This also ties into peer pressure.

Remember the question you most likely were asked as a teenager, "If all your friends jumped off a cliff, would you do it, too?" That might even be a question you have posed to your own children. In addition to jumping on the bandwagon and having a need to conform, peer pressure is also a real factor that impacts how we view products and even how we make decisions. In Arizona, as Covid-19 vaccinations became widely available, digital freeway signs started to display the number of vaccinated Arizonians. Instead of simply urging people to get the vaccine, the message stated, "7.8 million doses and counting. Get vaccinated." In other words, millions of people have already done it. Why don't you do it, too?

There is a lot of research on peer pressure and how it impacts our behaviors even as adults. A research team in Norway found that people increased their individual tips when their dining companions left a higher tip.[11] Based on the findings, the probability of you leaving a higher tip because your friend did, or vice versa, increases. When talking about peer pressure, we also need to consider how people conform to others.

A restaurant chain in Beijing brought in a group of researchers to uncover how the restaurant could improve the sales of certain dishes on the menu.[12] When you are dealing with a thick menu containing 60 hot dishes, this is no easy feat. However, the researchers were able to add a simple fix to the menu that significantly increased sales for five menu items.

The research team conducted multiple experiments, including one that randomly exposed diners to the top five popular dishes that displayed the number of plates sold in the previous week. The researchers were examining two different effects: saliency and observational learning. "Saliency" simply refers to a stimulus of some sort that stands out from the rest, which is a concept that is prevalent in cognitive psychology. According to this theory, diners seeing what other people chose from the menu can make those dishes stand out. However, a server mentioning sample dishes also has the potential to evoke the saliency effect. "Observational learning" in the context of this study means diners might choose popular dishes based on the mere observation of other diners' selections. There is one last concept thrown into the mix of this study you should know, which is "conformity." Based on the concept of conformity, individuals might choose the observed menu selections of other diners *because* they want to conform to the other diners' behavior.

So, what happened when diners saw the top five dishes? The demand for the top five popular dishes went up by an average of 13 percent to 20 percent, which can be attributed to the conformity concept. That's not a bad result considering the only change was a label on the menu indicating popularity. What an easy tactic for any business to do, not just a restaurant.

## IT'S FLYING OUT OF HERE!

If you are on social media for even a minute, you are exposed to marketing messages that highlight the popularity of products or services. The messages are often subtle, such as "back in stock" or "only a few tickets left." These statements indicate high demand and activate FOMO, which we discussed earlier in the book. We don't want to miss out on what everyone else is doing or buying.

Nordstrom, like many other retailers, highlights new products in its social media feeds. One such post promoted two new styles of its Nike Air shoe. Soon after the post went live, there was a flurry of comments, and a lot had to do with the items' availability. One customer asked about the availability in his store because his size was sold out online. What was Nordstrom's response? Basically, an apology and statement that if the shoe was sold out online, it was also sold out in the stores—with no chance of a restock. In other words, that shopper had already missed out. The shoe was in popular demand, and it was too late for him to get his own.

Home shopping networks have been using popular demand for decades. Shoppers can see in real time how many products have been sold, which creates FOMO.

QVC (which stands for quality, value, convenience) has been able to adapt in a marketplace dominated by Amazon and maintain its position in the home shopping arena. The QVC channel promotes 770 products every week on air in the United States, and the average shopper spends over $1,200 annually on QVC products.[13] QVC boasts that unlike buying from other online retailers, buying from QVC is a social experience, not a transaction. What has made QVC, and other home shopping networks, so successful is not only the social experience, but also the use of scarcity tactics.

One morning, QVC host Pat James-Dementri stood next to a clothing rack featuring a blouse and tank-top set. She told viewers that if they ordered now, they would get 30 percent off (time-related scarcity) and urged them not to wait. Behind the scenes, one of the producers was monitoring two screens: one showed call volume, and the other showed the colors and sizes left. Apparently the wine-colored blouse was the most popular that morning. A real-time dashboard assisted in boosting the sense of urgency with shoppers. The producer whispered into James-Dementri's earpiece that the wine color was in high demand. In a cheery voice that reached nearly 100 million homes, James-Dementri exclaimed, "The wine is flying out of here!"[14] And that it did, especially with that proclamation from the host.

While many people associate QVC with an older demographic, the company has taken steps to attract a wider audience. After purchasing its rival, the Home Shopping Network (HSN), QVC became the third largest e-commerce retailer in North America, only behind Walmart and Amazon.

Scarcity can be seen throughout the QVC website. "Trending" is a page located within the main navigation. Once on the page, you see a headline, "Trending on Q: See what has everyone buzzing." This is high demand in action. And QVC also does something not all online retailers do: it includes a "wait list."

Because home shopping networks have done such a great job incorporating scarcity, I wanted to talk with someone firsthand who had experience in that field. Who better to talk to about scarcity than Kevin Harrington? Remember from Chapter 1 that Kevin is an original "shark" on the TV show *Shark Tank*, creator of the infomercial, and pioneer of the As Seen On TV industry. As we started to talk about scarcity in marketing, Kevin brought up his early days with the Home Shopping Network. Both HSN and QVC sell other people's products and order inventory in advance of a special event. For instance, HSN will order 5,000 units of a product; therefore, when the hosts tell you, "We only have 5,000 to sell," they mean it.

Over the years, people would frequently ask Kevin whether these types of claims were true or not on HSN. Statements such as "Once it's gone, it's gone" can seem like a marketing tactic to push more products, but in the case of HSN, it is 100 percent accurate. Not only are there laws to adhere to within marketing (including truth-in-advertising laws, which set guidelines for what claims can be made by marketers), but the statements about products running out are meant to be more informative than persuasive. The scarcity situation in the shopping channel business is created because of the model of purchasing a certain quantity of products in advance. So why does this model work?

Imagine you're sitting comfortably in your living room, casually watching a shopping channel. A product is featured that has caught your attention. The host explains that there are 1,000 left, but then pauses as she gets the updated numbers and then says,

"Wait, there are only 95 pieces left." Now you are sitting upright watching the show, seriously considering whether you should buy the product. You continue to watch for the next 10 minutes, and then the host suddenly warns everyone, "We only have 5 left!" Then the host adds one more proclamation: "We may not bring this item back ever, and if we do, it still might not be for three or six months from now." What would you do?

From what we already know about the influence of scarcity, there is a strong likelihood that you would instantly move past the consideration stage of the purchase decision process and buy right then and there. *That* is the magic of scarcity in action.

You were exposed to supply-related scarcity (there are only a certain number available), demand-related scarcity (they're selling out fast because their popular), and time-related scarcity (you can only buy the products for a set period of time). In the end, the fear of missing out was too strong to ignore.

## AVOID DECEPTION

Out of all the types of scarcity, demand-related scarcity has been the one most associated with deception because it's easy to manipulate. It's one thing to have supplies running out because the item is truly popular. It's another to simply change the wording on an advertisement to make someone *think* the item is popular, even if it isn't. Marketers walk a fine line when purposely limiting quantities in an attempt to create scarcity. And when a person recognizes that the scarcity appeal is manipulated and fake, the appeal can negatively impact the perception of the product or brand.

Revisiting our earlier example of the luxury condominiums, what would happen if a potential buyer made an appointment to view the 10 percent available units left, only to discover that half of the condos were still available for sale? Most certainly the potential buyer would not purchase a unit and would view that company as deceptive. He would most likely share his experience with others and spread the word about the deceptive practice. The big lesson for marketers is to be very careful in using popular demand. There should not be a situation where high demand is fabricated.

## SCARCITY FROM DEMAND

There are other ways to communicate popularity in an ethical and truthful manner. Let's look at those together now.

### SALES RESTRICTIONS

Sales restrictions fall into the demand category. Let's say you are at the grocery store and see a great deal on cereal. You decide to buy a box, but then notice a sign that says "limit of 3 per customer." Just by reading the sign, you assume this promotion is causing high demand, so you buy the max of three instead of one. You don't want to miss out!

This technique has been so successful that stores continue to use it repeatedly. Remember the study from Chapter 2 that analyzed the sales figures for a large grocery chain in the United States and found that over an 80-week period, products that had a sales restriction like this sold significantly more units.[15] The next time a business has a sale, it might be wise to add a limit to the amount that can be purchased.

## BESTSELLERS

Lists of bestselling items, from books to cosmetics to music, have a strong influence on us because they signal popularity. When in doubt about what to buy, you will more than likely be drawn to the item that is mentioned to be a bestseller. This distinction helps us slip into the mindless decision-making mode, because while bestsellers aren't always scarce, they do communicate high demand and high sales.

Imagine that you walk into a large bookstore without a clear idea of the book you want to purchase. You could spend hours aimlessly walking down the aisles of books, or you could head straight to the displays that say "Bestsellers." If you choose one of those books, you are defaulting to the mentality of "that many buyers can't be wrong."

My colleague Janet explained her experience with a bestseller. Janet and her husband had just replaced the back patio door and wanted to upgrade their window covering. They decided to go with custom curtains. When the window covering representative sat down with Janet to go over fabric options, the representative made a comment that one fabric in particular was a bestseller among home designers. From that moment on, Janet was only interested in that "bestselling" fabric and chose not to look at the other options.

Products or services designated as "most popular" have the same effect, because in essence, it is the same message: everyone else is buying it, so it must be great.

From a business perspective, spotlighting the most popular or bestselling products or services will evoke FOMO because we don't want to be left out. It will also create a sense of confidence in making a purchase decision, because if something is in high demand, it must be good. By labeling something as "bestselling" or "most popular," you're giving that product a special stamp of approval.

## BACK IN STOCK

Showing that a product is now back in stock implies that it is popular and has sold out before. This is a simple and very popular tactic because all it requires is that you display a sign saying a product is available for purchase again. Some companies, such as UNIQLO, Ugg, and Williams Sonoma, even send out email reminders to let customers know the news.

## NUMBER OF ITEMS LEFT

In Chapter 5, we looked at Erica's experience with a website that sold beauty products. The story illustrated an unethical approach to scarcity that should be avoided. What we didn't get into is why the "Only 1 left" statement on the product page caused Erica to urgently make her purchase. So let's get into that now.

Even if an item is not scarce, showing low levels of inventory, such as "only three left," triggers the same effect as scarcity.[16] One study tested this theory by tracking sales of 35,000 print books on a large e-commerce site. For each product page, basic information such as price, rating, date of product launch, and sales rank was listed. Additionally, the product pages included a scarcity message showing the available stock and a dispatch cutoff time (e.g., "Order within the next $x$ hours to get the good tomorrow"). After two weeks of tracking and later analyzing the data, the research team concluded that adding a scarcity message indicating the amount of units left prompted sales, but mainly when the customers were further along in the purchase process. This means they had moved from casual browsing to more intentional shopping. This demonstrates an opportunity for businesses that either sell in the online space or promote products or services on their websites. Indicating how many units are left can promote higher sales, but make sure the statement is true and accurate.

Outside of the retail world, popular demand has worked well for service-oriented businesses. Simple statements on websites that show how many clients have been served, or show which companies have become clients, will elicit a perception of popularity. Even more than that, though, salespeople who make comments such as, "We are only taking on two more clients," activate demand-related scarcity and a fear of missing out.

Booking.com continues to be a great example of how to use this type of limited-availability scarcity. When this multibillion-dollar company first included information about the limited number of rooms available at each hotel for a certain price, reservations went through the roof. The number jumped so significantly that the customer service team thought it was a system error.[17] However, it was the powerful effect of scarcity that had caused bookings to skyrocket. When customers could see the limited opportunity to purchase the room at the low advertised price, it caused a sense of urgency.

*Note:* Similar to showing how many items are left, another approach in high-demand scarcity is to show the number of items sold. For example, a website might show how many times a hotel has been booked that day or how many units of a product have already been sold.

## WAIT LIST

A wait list is not only an indication that a product is in high demand, but also an opportunity for the people on the list to still get the hot product . . . they just have to be patient. In 2003, Banana Republic heavily promoted a $198 jacket, which created demand.[18] However, the retailer then limited the shipments to about half of the normal run, creating a flood of wait lists. There are many more examples of companies using wait lists to signal high demand, including car companies, golf club manufacturers, private schools, apartment complexes, and other nonretailer organizations. Robinhood, the zero-commission stock trading app, had a wait list of nearly 1 million people a year before it launched. Robinhood took the wait-list approach again in 2018 and announced a wait list for commission-free cryptocurrency trading. Within one day, the list grew to over 1,250,000 people.[19]

If all these companies and industries can successfully signal high demand for products and services, why not create a wait list prior to launch and do the same? Let customers know that there is a good possibility of the product or service running out (again) based on demand. Or depending on the release date, simply communicate that those on the wait list get the product or service before everyone else.

---

As we have learned, scarcity of all kinds can serve a business well because it indicates competition and social acceptance and results in a perceived higher product value than an item that is not in high demand.

The question now becomes, where do we go next with what we know?

## KEY SELLING POINTS

- When an item is scarce because of high demand versus other circumstances (like limited supply or time), the perceived value is even stronger.

- This form of scarcity creates a feeling of urgency, based on the belief that once the products are sold out, the chance to own the product is gone forever.

- Scarcity due to high demand propels us to do something immediately.

- Scarcity that is caused by demand entices people who want to feel included and/or identify with a certain group.

- By promoting sales restrictions, bestsellers, back-in-stock products, current items left, or the need to sign up on a wait list, a business can ignite the behaviors that result from scarcity.

# CHAPTER 10

# Where Do We Go from Here?

"Oscar Mayer comes out with bologna-inspired sheet masks," shouted the headline on Today.com.[1] Yes, you read that right. Oscar Mayer, the meat company known for its bologna and catchy song "My bologna has a first name, it's O-S-C-A-R," created a limited-edition face mask in partnership with Korean beauty company Seoul Mamas. The mask appealed to people who remember those times as children biting holes for eyes and a mouth, then slapping the bologna right to their face. The idea was to create smiles for Oscar Mayer fans and beauty enthusiasts. Instead of the meat used in that fun childhood tradition, though, the masks were composed of "a hydrating and restoring hydrogel" and were intended to "promote skin elasticity, improve hydration and moisture retention, offer anti-inflammatory benefits, and provide protection for the skin," according to a Kraft Heinz news release. The face mask was priced at $4.99 and sold on Amazon.com. Within hours of the product's release, it was sold out.

In a news statement, Kraft Heinz explained that demand was higher than expected for the face mask, which became Amazon's #1 new release in the Beauty & Personal Care category and the #3 top-selling face mask—within just 12 hours of launching. Kraft Heinz went on to explain that it was working diligently with the seller and Amazon to get the sheet masks restocked within the coming days. In the meantime, customers were told to add the mask to their Amazon Wish List and/or continue to check back for availability.

The release of the Oscar Mayer face mask stirred up nostalgic feelings among customers, but it also triggered the psychological components of scarcity. Oscar Mayer created multiple Instagram posts, including one shortly after the product launch and sellout announcing that it would be restocking on Amazon in the coming days. By using the word "restocking," that one particular post caused all types of comments from fans, many of which expressed FOMO and a strong desire to get their hands on the mask. Various news outlets, including *USA Today*, reported on the mask's unavailability and coming restock.[2]

When we break down the sellout of the Oscar Mayer face mask, we see many of the theories we have been exploring in the previous chapters. The news reported both before and after the mask sold out, touting it as a *limited-edition product* with *limited supplies*—providing us with a credible source. Furthermore, we have seen that when people believe others are going to be influenced by a message, they will take action immediately. Customers jumped on purchasing their masks via Amazon.com. Finally, because it was clear that the mask was a limited-edition item and only here for a short time with limited supply, those who desire uniqueness would be drawn to it. Additionally, what the brand did well was promote its mask in advance, raising excitement and a sense of fun within its community.

You might not sell face masks designed to look like bologna, but there is a lot you can gain by following Oscar Mayer's example and the example of the companies and case studies we've learned about in the previous chapters. You can use *limited-edition* and *supply-related scarcity*, like Oscar Mayer did, or focus on *demand-related scarcity*, similar to what QVC does. Or you can follow the examples of Starbucks and Kohl's and implement *time-related scarcity*.

The stories, tactics, and strategies we've come to understand should now act as your guide to determine how you sell going forward, including which type of scarcity appeal to use, when to use it, and how to implement it ethically.

## SCARCITY AFFECTS US ALL AND RUNS DEEP

When I would tell people I was working on a book about scarcity, 9 times out of 10 they would quickly tell me that they had a story that aligned with my material. For example, I would hear about a time they waited in line outside a store for a chance at a limited-supply item or how they joined a club just because it was exclusive. The stories ranged from major purchases to minor ones, but what became apparent to me is that they didn't realize they were basing their decisions on scarcity. In fact, they hadn't really stopped to consider what was driving their decisions. I can attest to this being the case in all the personal stories I shared, too. Not only do we not realize that we are exposed so frequently to messages of scarcity, but we often don't recognize that it is causing us to take action.

Maybe that was you before reading this book. But I bet you see things a little differently now.

When I initially started researching scarcity, I thought I had a decent understanding of how it affected people, especially consumers. However, I quickly realized that scarcity is complex and has many layers. It is a subject that has fascinated researchers for decades and resulted in countless studies, and the end results are clear: scarcity influences us and makes us want to buy, even if we aren't aware of it.

Scarcity is not a simple concept and is more than supply versus demand. Different types of scarcity have different effects and are more influential in certain groups. For instance, if you have a luxury good and are targeting people who want to distinguish themselves from everyone else, then the focus should be on limited supply versus high demand. The opposite is true if you are targeting consumers who have a strong desire to conform because they will want popular items and will be drawn to products that have limited availability due to demand.

Scarcity has multiple layers and complexities. In some scenarios, exposure to scarcity might cause us to make a quick decision or take a mental shortcut. In other situations, we'll reach for the product on the shelf that looks nearly out of stock instead of a similar product that has an abundance of quantity.

## BUILD LOYALTY, CULTIVATE COMMUNITIES, AND DEEPEN RELATIONSHIPS

Scarcity can be a catalyst in increasing revenue. It's something I have learned through research and practice. Yet as I have continued to dive deeper into my research through interviews with customers and executives at various brands, it has become clear that scarcity can have other positive consequences that are less obvious, but no less powerful.

McDonald's sporadically releases limited-time products, such as the McRib, and creates engagement and fun among customers. Lectric eBikes generates excitement and the anticipation caused by the customer wait list. Harry & David cultivates communities by bringing customers together into exclusive groups with access to limited-supply products.

Scarcity is one of the most powerful influence tactics in the world, and that power can change the course of a business and propel professional success. Let the words of Winston Churchill stay with you as you consider just how and when you might apply the incredible power of scarcity going forward:

**Where there is great power, there is great responsibility.**

# Scarcity Definitions at a Glance

**Demand-related scarcity.** Scarcity that occurs when a product is in short supply because of its popularity and the high demand for it.

**Limited-edition scarcity.** A type of *supply-related scarcity*. Scarcity is "built in"—the number of units produced is deliberately limited. A limited-edition product is typically a slightly modified version of the regular product. Limited-edition products cater to the desire for exclusivity.

**Supply-related scarcity.** Scarcity that occurs when there are not that many products available due to a shortage, and so each time a customer purchases the scarce item, the remaining number of items for purchase decreases.

**Time-related scarcity.** Scarcity that occurs when there is a restriction on the time the product is available for purchase.

# Notes

## Introduction

1. https://www.nytimes.com/1996/12/22/nyregion/elmo-the-spirit-of-christmas.html.
2. Kastrenakes, J. "Beeple Sold an NFT for $69 Million." *The Verge*, March 11, 2021. https://www.theverge.com/2021/3/11/22325054/beeple-christies-nft-sale-cost-everydays-69-million.

## Chapter 1

1. Kanfer, S. *The Last Empire: De Beers, Diamonds, and the World*. New York: Noonday Press, 1995.
2. Friedman, U. "How an Ad Campaign Invented the Diamond Engagement Ring." *The Atlantic*, February 13, 2015. Retrieved from https://www.theatlantic.com/international/archive/2015/02/how-an-ad-campaign-invented-the-diamond-engagement-ring/385376/.
3. John, M., Melis, A. P., Read, D., Rossano, F., and Tomasello, M. "The Preference for Scarcity: A Developmental and Comparative Perspective." *Psychology & Marketing* 35, no. 8 (2018), 603–615. doi:10.1002/mar.21109.
4. Huijsmans, I., Ma, I., Micheli, L., Civai, C., Stallen, M., and Sanfey, A. G. "A Scarcity Mindset Alters Neural Processing Underlying Consumer Decision Making." *Proceedings of the National Academy of Sciences* 116, no. 24 (2019), 11699–11704. https://doi.org/10.1073/pnas.1818572116.

5. Kwon, W., Deshpande, G., Katz, J., and Byun, S. "What Does the Brain Tell About Scarcity Bias? Cognitive Neuroscience Evidence of Decision Making Under Scarcity." *International Textile and Apparel Association Annual Conference Proceedings* 74, no. 41 (2017). https://doi.org/10.31274/itaa_proceedings-180814-374.

6. Morrison, M., "Secret McRib Network Defunct as McD's Rolls It Out Nationwide." *Advertising Age* 81, no. 39 (2010), 3–24.

## Chapter 2

1. Pennebaker, J. W., Dyer, M. A., Caulkins, R. S., Litowitz, D. L., Ackreman, P. L., Anderson, D. B., et al. "Don't the Girls Get Prettier at Closing Time: A Country and Western Application to Psychology." *Personality and Social Psychology Bulletin* 5, no.1 (1979), 122–125.

2. Brehm, J. W. *A Theory of Psychological Reactance.* New York: Academic Press, 1966.

3. Rosenberg, B. D., and Siegel, J. T. "A 50-Year Review of Psychological Reactance Theory: Do Not Read This Article." *Motivation Science* 4, no. 4 (2018), 281–300. doi:10.1037mot0000091.

4. Zemack-Rugar, Y., Moore, S. G., and Fitzsimons, G. J. "Just Do It! Why Committed Consumers React Negatively to Assertive Ads." *Journal of Consumer Psychology* 27, no. 3 (2017), 287–301. doi:10.1016/j.jcps.2017.01.002.

5. Rummel, A., Howard, J., Swinton, J. M., and Seymour, D. B. "You Can't Have That! A Study of Reactance Effects & Children's Consumer Behavior." *Journal of Marketing Theory and Practice* 8, no. 1 (2000), 38–45.

6. Kowarski, I. "11 Colleges with the Lowest Acceptance Rates." *US News*, November 10, 2020. https://www.usnews.com/education/best-colleges/the-short-list-college/articles/colleges-with-the-lowest-acceptance-rates.

7. Levitz, J., and Korn, M. "How Rick Singer's 'Side Door' Worked in College Admissions Scandal." *Wall Street Journal*, September 22, 2021. https://www.wsj.com/articles/how-rick-singers-side-door-worked-in-college-admissions-scandal-11632312003?mod=article_inline.

8. Lartey, J. "Felicity Huffman Among Dozens Charged over Admissions Fraud at Top US Schools." *The Guardian*, March 12, 2019. https://www.theguardian.com/us-news/2019/mar/12/us-college-admissions-fraud-scheme-charges-georgetown-southern-california-universities.

9.   Drell, C. "What Is the College Admissions Scandal? Lori Loughlin and Felicity Huffman Were Indicted." *Marie Claire*, March 15, 2019, https://www.marieclaire.com/politics/a26801201/college-admissions-bribery-scandal-felicity-huffman-lori-loughlin/.

10.  Hathcock, M. "Say Goodbye to Hobby Lobby's 40% off Coupon." *The Krazy Coupon Lady* blog. TheKrazyCouponLady.com, February 12, 2021. https://thekrazycouponlady.com/tips/couponing/hobby-lobby-discontinuing-40-off-coupon.

11.  "KCL Press." The Krazy Coupon Lady. Accessed January 22, 2022. https://thekrazycouponlady.com/press.

12.  Hathcock. "Say Goodbye to Hobby Lobby's 40% off Coupon."

13.  "Hobby Lobby Eliminates Its Famous 40% off Coupons." Coupons in the News, January 28, 2021. https://couponsinthenews.com/2021/01/28/hobby-lobby-eliminates-its-famous-40-off-coupons/.

14.  Birnbaum, G. E., Zholtack, K., and Reis, H. T. "No Pain, No Gain: Perceived Partner Mate Value Mediates the Desire-Inducing Effect of Being Hard-to-Get During Online and Face-to-Face Encounters." *Journal of Social and Personal Relationships* (2020).

15.  Griskevicius, V., Goldstein, N. J., Mortensen, C. R., Sundie, J. M., Cialdini, R. B., and Kenrick, D. T. "Fear and Loving in Las Vegas: Evolution, Emotion, and Persuasion." *Journal of Marketing Research* 46, no. 3 (2009), 384–395.

16.  Hamilton, R., Thompson, D., Bone, S., Chaplin, L. N., Griskevicius, V., Goldsmith, K., et al. "The Effects of Scarcity on Consumer Decision Journeys." *Journal of the Academy of Marketing Science* 47, no. 3 (2019), 532–550. doi:10.1007/s11747-018-0604-7.

17.  Griskevicius, Goldstein, Mortensen, Sundie, Cialdini, and Kenrick. "Fear and Loving in Las Vegas."

18.  Inman, J. J., Peter, A. C., and Raghubir, P. "Framing the Deal: The Role of Restrictions in Accentuating Deal Value." *Journal of Consumer Research* 24, no. 1 (1997), 68–79. https://doi-org.lopes.idm.oclc.org/10.1086/209494.

19.  Wansink, Brian, Kent, Robert J., and Hoch, Stephen J. "An Anchoring and Adjustment Model of Purchase Quantity Decisions." *Journal of Marketing Research* 35, no. 1 (1998), 71–81. doi:10.2307/3151931.

20.  Johnco, C., Wheeler, L., and Taylor, A. "They Do Get Prettier at Closing Time: A Repeated Measures Study of the Closing-Time Effect and Alcohol." *Social Influence* 5, no. 4 (2010), 261–271. https://doi-org.lopes.idm.oclc.org/10.1080/15534510.2010.487650.

## Chapter 3

1.  Wansink, B., and Sobal, J. "Mindless Eating: The 200 Daily Food Decisions We Overlook." *Environment and Behavior* 39, no.1 (2007), 106–123.

2.  Yarrow, K. *Decoding the New Consumer Mind: How and Why We Shop and Buy.* San Francisco: Jossey-Bass, 2014.

3.  Jackson, T., Dawson, R., and Wilson, D. "The Cost of Email Interruption." *Journal of Systems and Information Technology* 5, no. 1 (2001), 81–92. https://doi.org/10.1108/13287260180000 760.

4.  Zhu, M., and Ratner, R. K. "Scarcity Polarizes Preferences: The Impact on Choice Among Multiple Items in a Product Class." *Journal of Marketing Research* 52, no. 1 (2015), 13–26.

5.  Adams, K. "Famous Kentucky Whiskey Heist 'Pappygate' Coming to Netflix in New Documentary." *Louisville Courier Journal*, July 20, 2021. https://www.courier-journal.com/story/entertainment/ movies/2021/06/24/netflix-documentary-series-features-kentucky -pappygate-whiskey-heist/5318783001/.

6.  Hall, G. A. "Rare Kentucky Bourbon Stolen in Apparent Inside Job." *USA Today*, October 16, 2013. https://www.usatoday.com/ story/money/business/2013/10/16/pappy-van-winkle-bourbon -stolen/2997065/.

7.  Associated Press. "'Pappygate' Ringleader Gets Time in Prison . . . Where There's No Bourbon." *Courier Journal*, June 1, 2018. https://www.courier-journal.com/story/news/2018/06/01/ kentucky-bourbon-pappy-van-winkle-theft-ringleader-sentenced -prison/663923002/.

8.  Costello, D. "Judge's Order Lets 'Pappygate' Ringleader out of Prison After 30 Days." *Courier Journal*, June 29, 2018. https://www .courier-journal.com/story/news/crime/2018/06/29/pappygate -leader-released-prison-after-30-days/746225002/.

9.  Romano, A. "Bruno Mars' Las Vegas Shows Sold Out in Minutes—Here's How You Can Still Attend." *Travel + Leisure*, May 6, 2021. https://www.travelandleisure.com/trip-ideas/bruno -mars-park-mgm-hotel-las-vegas-package.

10. Schoormans, J. P. L., and Robben, H. S. J. "The Effect of New Package Design on Product Attention, Categorization, and Evaluation." *Journal of Economic Psychology* 18 (1997), 271–287.

11. Brannon, L. A., and Brock, T. C. "Limiting Time for Responding Enhances Behavior Corresponding to the Merits of Compliance Appeals: Refutations of Heuristic-Cue Theory in Service and

Consumer Settings." *Journal of Consumer Psychology* 10, no. 3 (2001), 135–146. doi:10.1207/s15327663jcp1003_2.

12. Goldsmith, R. E., Lafferty, B. A., and Newell, S. J. "The Impact of Corporate Credibility and Celebrity Credibility on Consumer Reaction to Advertisements and Brands." *Journal of Advertising* 29, no. 3 (2000), 43–54. doi:10.1080/00913367.2000.10673616.

13. Engelmann, J. B., Capra, C. M., Noussair, C., and Berns, G.S. "Expert Financial Advice Neurobiologically 'Offloads' Financial Decision-Making Under Risk." *PLoS ONE* 4, no. 3 (2009), e4957. doi:10.1371/journal.pone.0004957.

14. DeLamater, J. D., Myers, D. J., and Collett, J. L. *Social Psychology.* Boulder, CO: Westview, 2015.

15. Klucharev, V., Smidts, A., and Guillén, F. "Brain Mechanisms of Persuasion: How 'Expert Power' Modulates Memory and Attitudes." *Social Cognitive & Affective Neuroscience* 3, no. 4 (2008), 353–366. doi:10.1093/scan/nsn022.

## Chapter 4

1. Mellers, B. A., Yin, S., and Berman, J. Z. "Reconciling Loss Aversion and Gain Seeking in Judged Emotions." *Current Directions in Psychological Science* 30, no. 2 (2021), 95–102. doi:10.1177/0963721421992043.

2. DeLamater, J. D., Myers, D. J., and Collett, J. L. *Social Psychology.* Boulder, CO: Westview, 2015.

3. Mellers, Yin, and Berman. "Reconciling Loss Aversion and Gain Seeking in Judged Emotions."

4. DeLamater, Myers, and Collett. *Social Psychology.*

5. Charpentier, C. J., De Martino, B., Sim, A. L., Sharot, T., and Roiser, J. P. "Emotion-Induced Loss Aversion and Striatal-Amygdala Coupling in Low-Anxious Individuals." *Social Cognitive & Affective Neuroscience* 11, no. 4 (April 2016), 569–579. doi:10.1093/scan/nsv139.

6. Bar-Hillel, M., and Neter, E. "Why Are People Reluctant to Exchange Lottery Tickets?" *Journal of Personality and Social Psychology* 70, no. 1 (1996), 17–27.

7. Risen, J. L., and Gilovich, T. "Another Look at Why People Are Reluctant to Exchange Lottery Tickets." *Journal of Personality and Social Psychology* 93, no. 1 (2007), 12–22.

8. Kahneman, D., and Tversky, A. "Prospect Theory: An Analysis of Decision Under Risk." *Econometrica* 47, no. 2 (1979), 263–292.

9. Seaton, P. "'I Hate to Lose More Than I Love to Win.' How Jimmy Connors Refused to Go Away." CalvinAyre.com, February 28,

2020. https://calvinayre.com/2020/02/28/sports/i-hate-to-lose
-more-than-i-love-to-win-how-jimmy-connors-refused-to-go
-away/.

10. Dalakas, V., and Stewart, K. "Earning Extra Credit or Losing
Extra Credit? A Classroom Experiment on Framing Incentives
as Gains or Losses." *Atlantic Marketing Journal* 9, no. 1 (2020),
44–55.

11. Inman, J. J., Peter, A. C., and Raghubir, P. "Framing the
Deal: The Role of Restrictions in Accentuating Deal Value."
*Journal of Consumer Research* 24, no. 1 (1997), 68–79.
doi:10.1086/209494.

12. Abendroth, L. J., and Diehl, K. "Now or Never: Effects of Limited
Purchase Opportunities on Patterns of Regret over Time." *Journal
of Consumer Research* 33, no. 3 (2006), 342–351. https://doi-org
.lopes.idm.oclc.org/10.1086/508438.

13. Lange, D. "Magic Kingdom Walt Disney World Florida
Attendance 2019." *Statista*, November 30, 2020. https://www
.statista.com/statistics/232966/attendance-at-the-walt-disney
-world-magic-kingdom-theme-park/.

14. Byun, S., and Sternquist, B. "Here Today, Gone Tomorrow:
Consumer Reactions to Perceived Limited Availability." *Journal
of Marketing Theory and Practice* 20, no. 2 (2012), 223–234.
doi:10.2753/MTP1069-6679200207.

## Chapter 5

1. Crouth, G. "Spa Client Manipulated into Bum Deal Irate."
*Pretoria News* (South Africa). November 13, 2020.

2. Freeman, L. "The Marketing 100: Beanie Babies: Ty Warner." *Ad
Age*, June 30, 1997. https://adage.com/article/news/marketing-
100-beanie-babies-ty-warner/71576.

3. Bissonnette, Z. *The Great Beanie Baby Bubble: Mass Delusion
and the Dark Side of Cute.* New York: Portfolio/Penguin, 2015.

4. Hunt, E. "What Beanie Babies Taught a Generation About the
Horrors of Boom and Bust." *The Guardian*, June 19, 2019. https://
www.theguardian.com/lifeandstyle/shortcuts/2019/jun/19/what-
beanie-babies-taught-a-generation-about-the-horrors-of-boom-
and-bust.

5. "Reported Retirement Sparks Beanie Buzz." *Ad Age*, September 13,
1999. https://adage.com/article/news/reported-retirement-sparks
-beanie-buzz/61176.

6. Ibid.

7.  Dwyer, J. "Clothing Retailer Says It Will No Longer Destroy Unworn Garments." *New York Times*, January 7, 2010. https://www.nytimes.com/2010/01/07/nyregion/07clothes.html.

8.  Mohr, S., Kühl, R. "Exploring Persuasion Knowledge in Food Advertising: An Empirical Analysis." *SN Bus Econ* 1, 107 (2021). https://doi.org/10.1007/s43546-021-00108-y.

9.  Haugtvedt, C. P., Herr, P. M., and Kardes, F. R., eds. *Handbook of Consumer Psychology*. New York: Lawrence Erlbaum Associates, 2008.

10. Ibid.

11. Friestad, M., and Wright, P. "The Persuasion Knowledge Model: How People Cope with Persuasion Attempts." *Journal of Consumer Research* 21, no. 1 (1994), 1. https://doi.org/10.1086/209380.

12. Haugtvedt, Herr, and Kardes, eds. *Handbook of Consumer Psychology*.

13. Reuters Staff. "Global Auto Recovery to Take More Hits from Japan Chip Plant Fire, Severe U.S. Weather: IHS." *Reuters*, March 31, 2021. https://www.reuters.com/article/us-autos-chips/global-auto-recovery-to-take-more-hits-from-japan-chip-plant-fire-severe-u-s-weather-ihs-idUSKBN2BN27E.

14. Alba, J. W., Mela, C. F., Shimp, T. A., and Urbany, J. E. "The Effect of Discount Frequency and Depth on Consumer Price Judgments." *Journal of Consumer Research* 26, no. 2 (1999), 99–114.

15. Hardesty, D. M., Bearden, W. O., and Carlson. J. P. "Persuasion Knowledge and Consumer Reactions to Pricing Tactics." *Journal of Retailing* 83, no. 2 (2007), 199–210. doi:10.1016/j.jretai.2006.06.003.

16. Alba, Mela, Shimp, and Urbany. "The Effect of Discount Frequency and Depth on Consumer Price Judgments."

17. Drolet, A., and Yoon, C., eds. *The Aging Consumer: Perspectives from Psychology and Economics*. London: Taylor & Francis Group, 2010. ProQuest Ebook Central.

18. Ziaei, M., and Fischer, H. "Emotion and Aging: The Impact of Emotion on Attention, Memory, and Face Recognition in Late Adulthood." In J. R. Absher and J. Cloutier (eds.). *Neuroimaging Personality, Social Cognition, and Character*. London: Elsevier, 2016, pp. 259–278. https://doi.org/10.1016/b978-0-12-800935-2.00013-0.

19. Phillips, L. W., and Sternthal, B. "Age Differences in Information Processing: A Perspective on the Aged Consumer." *Journal of*

*Marketing Research* 14, no. 4 (1977), 444–457. doi:10.2307/3151185.

20. Kaur, D., Mustika, M. Dwi, and Sjabadhyni, B. "Affect or Cognition: Which Is More Influencing Older Adult Consumers' Loyalty?" *Heliyon* 4, no. 4 (2018). https://doi.org/10.1016/j.heliyon.2018.e00610.

21. "What Drives Brand Loyalty Today." *Morning Consult*. Accessed August 3, 2021. https://morningconsult.com/form/brand-loyalty-today/.

22. Drolet and Yoon, eds. *The Aging Consumer*.

23. Riggle, E. D., and Johnson, M. M. "Age Difference in Political Decision Making: Strategies for Evaluating Political Candidates." *Political Behavior* 18, no. 1 (1996), 99–118. https://doi.org/10.1007/bf01498661.

24. Drolet and Yoon, eds. *The Aging Consumer*.

25. Fung, H. H., and Carstensen, L. L. "Sending Memorable Messages to the Old: Age Differences in Preferences and Memory for Advertisements." *Journal of Personality and Social Psychology* 85, no. 1 (2003), 163–178.

## Chapter 6

1. McDonald's USA LLC. "Look Who's Back! McDonald's® Shamrock Shake® Returns to Mark the First Green of Spring." *PRNewswire*, February 2, 2021. https://www.prnewswire.com/news-releases/look-whos-back-mcdonalds-shamrock-shake-returns-to-mark-the-first-green-of-spring-301220153.html.

2. Godinho, S., Prada, M., and Garrido, M. V. "Under Pressure: An Integrative Perspective of Time Pressure Impact on Consumer Decision-Making." *Journal of International Consumer Marketing* 28, no. 4 (2016), 251–273. doi:10.1080/08961530.2016.1148654.

3. Aggarwal, P., and Vaidyanathan, R. "Use It or Lose It: Purchase Acceleration Effects on Time-Limited Promotions." *Journal of Consumer Behaviour* 2, no. 4 (2003), 393–403.

4. Gabler, C. B., and Reynolds, K. E. "Buy Now or Buy Later: The Effects of Scarcity and Discounts on Purchase Decisions." *Journal of Marketing Theory & Practice* 21, no. 4 (2013), 441–456. doi:10.2753/MTP1069-6679210407.

5. Aggarwal and Vaidyanathan. "Use It or Lose It."

6. Wu, Y., Xin, L., Li, D., Yu, J., and Guo J. "How Does Scarcity Promotion Lead to Impulse Purchase in the Online Market? A Field Experiment." *Information & Management* 58, no. 1 (2021). doi:10.1016/j.im.2020.103283.

7.  Song, M., Choi, S., and Moon, J. "Limited Time or Limited Quantity? The Impact of Other Consumer Existence and Perceived Competition on the Scarcity Messaging—Purchase Intention Relation." *Journal of Hospitality and Tourism Management* 47, no. 3 (June 2021),167–175. doi:10.1016/j.jhtm.2021.03.012.

8.  Prime Rib Specials (n.d.). Retrieved March 13, 2021, from https://www.bjsrestaurants.com/prime-rib-specials.

9.  Mims, C. "The Untold History of Starbucks' Pumpkin Spice Latte." *Quartz*. October 17, 2013. https://qz.com/136781/psl-untold-history-of-starbucks-pumpkin-spice-latte/.

10. Chou, J. "History of the Pumpkin Spice Latte." *The Daily Meal*. October 28, 2013. https://www.thedailymeal.com/news/history-pumpkin-spice-latte/102813.

11. Ibid.

12. Ibid.

13. Lucas, A. "Starbucks Is Introducing Its First New Pumpkin Coffee Beverage Since the Pumpkin Spice Latte." *CNBC*, August 26, 2019. https://www.cnbc.com/2019/08/26/starbucks-is-introducing-its-first-new-pumpkin-beverage-since-the-pumpkin-spice-latte.html.

14. Valinsky, J. "Attention Red Cup Fans! Here's How to Get Your Free Reusable Holiday Cup at Starbucks." *CNN Business*. ABC7 Los Angeles, November 18, 2021. https://abc7.com/starbucks-cups-reusable-cup-holiday/11250222/.

15. "Five-Day Flash Sale with Savings of Up to 60% for Your Staycation on Yas Island." *Adgully*, September 1, 2021.

16. Berezina, K., Semrad, K. J., Stepchenkova, S., and Cobanoglu, C. "The Managerial Flash Sales Dash: Is There Advantage or Disadvantage at the Finish Line?" *International Journal of Hospitality Management* 54 (April 2016),12–24. doi:10.1016/j.ijhm.2016.01.003.

17. Berezina, Semrad, Stepchenkova, and Cobanoglu. "The Managerial Flash Sales Dash."

18. Hobica, G. "Confessions of an Airline Revenue Manager." Fox News, November 15, 2015. https://www.foxnews.com/travel/confessions-of-an-airline-revenue-manager.

19. Dhawan, N. "J.Crew Just Launched a Huge Flash Sale with an Extra 60% off Sale Items—but Only for Today." *USA Today*, March 19, 2021. https://www.usatoday.com/story/tech/reviewedcom/2021/03/19/j-crew-sale-get-extra-60-off-sale-clothing-shoes-and-more/4765251001/.

20. Lunden, I. "Five Woot Execs Check Out, as Daily Deals Site Feels the Strain Under Owner Amazon." *TechCrunch*. May 12, 2013.

https://techcrunch.com/2013/05/12/five-woot-execs-check-out-as
-daily-deals-site-feels-the-strain-under-owner-amazon/.

21. Ibid.

22. Houston, J. "A Psychologist Explains How Trader Joe's Gets You to Spend More Money." *Business Insider.* January 22, 2021. https://www.businessinsider.com/trader-joes-how-gets-you-spend-money-psychologist-2019-1.

23. Gasparro, A. "Coupon-Clipping Fades into History as COVID-19 Accelerates Digital Shift." *Wall Street Journal*, September 1, 2020. https://www.wsj.com/articles/coupon-clipping-fades-into-history-as-covid-19-accelerates-digital-shift-11598702400.

24. "Integrated Print and Digital Promotion: 2020 Trends & Insights." *Kantar.* February 25, 2021. https://cdne.kantar.com/north-america/inspiration/advertising-media/print-and-digital-promotion-trends-2020.

25. Ibid.

26. Johnson, E. "How AI Is Transforming Coupon Marketing Campaigns?" *ClickZ*, January 26, 2021. https://www.clickz.com/how-ai-is-transforming-coupon-marketing-campaigns/264928/.

27. Smith, G. "Coupon Code Stats." *Blippr*, April 4, 2021. https://www.blippr.com/about/coupon-code-stats/.

28. Stuever, H. "TLC's 'Extreme Couponing': Little Piggies Go to Market, and Clean Up on Aisle 5." *Washington Post*, April 5, 2011. https://www.washingtonpost.com/lifestyle/style/tlcs-extreme-couponing-little-piggies-go-to-market-and-clean-up-on-aisle-5/2011/04/04/AFqJp9kC_story.html.

29. "Coupons.Com and Claremont Graduate University Study Reveals Coupons Make You Happier and More Relaxed." *Business Wire*, November 19, 2012. https://www.businesswire.com/news/home/20121119005572/en/Coupons.com-and-Claremont-Graduate-University-Study-Reveals-Coupons-Make-You-Happier-and-More-Relaxed.

30. Ibid.

31. Inman, J. J., Peter, A. C., and Raghubir, P. "Framing the Deal: The Role of Restrictions in Accentuating Deal Value." *Journal of Consumer Research* 24, no. 1 (1997), 68–79. doi:10.1086/209494.

32. Krishna, A., and Zhang, Z. J. "Short- or Long-Duration Coupons: The Effect of the Expiration Date on the Profitability of Coupon Promotions." *Management Science* 45, no. 8 (1999), 1041–1056.

33. Inman, Peter, and Raghubir. "Framing the Deal."

34. Sinha, I., Chandran, R., and Srinivasan, S. S. "Consumer Evaluations of Price and Promotional Restrictions—a Public Policy Perspective." *Journal of Public Policy & Marketing* 18, no. 1 (1999), 37–51. https://doi.org/10.1177/074391569901800106.

35. Hanna, R., Swain, S., and Berger, P. "Optimizing Time-Limited Price Promotions." *Journal of Marketing Analytics* 4, no. 2 (2016), 77–92. doi:10.1057/s41270-016-0006-y.

36. Rodriguez, A. "Getting to Know You: J.C. Penney, Kohl's Go for Personalization." *Advertising Age*, May 18, 2015.

37. "Disruptions in Retail Through Digital Transformation: Reimagining the Store of the Future." Deloitte, November 2017.

38. "About Us." Dunkin'. Accessed September 11, 2021. https://www.dunkindonuts.com/en/about/about-us.

39. Gasparro, A. "Coupon-Clipping Fades into History as COVID-19 Accelerates Digital Shift." *Wall Street Journal*, September 1, 2020. https://www.wsj.com/articles/coupon-clipping-fades-into-history -as-covid-19-accelerates-digital-shift-11598702400.

40. Johnson. "How AI Is Transforming Coupon Marketing Campaigns?"

41. "TrueShip Announces Limited-Time Sale: 50% Off First Month of ReadyShipper Shipping Software for New Users with Coupon Code RS-SAVE-50." *Marketwire Canada*, July 15, 2015.

42. "Nissan: Victoria Dealership Service Center Provides Select Maintenance Coupons for a Limited Time." *Contify Automotive News*, July 16, 2020. Gale General OneFile.

43. "BlueHost Coupon—Just $3.95 per Month, a Limited Time Offer." *PRWeb Newswire*, June 9, 2012. Gale General OneFile.

44. "Dell Back-to-School Coupon: Save $150 on XPS, Alienware, Inspiron," *ICT Monitor Worldwide*, July 22, 2017.

45. Email received from Joann.com on September 11, 2021.

46. Jcrew.com, September 10, 2021.

## Chapter 7

1. Rosenberg, E. "'The Shed at Dulwich' Was London's Top-Rated Restaurant. Just One Problem: It Didn't Exist." *Washington Post*, March 28, 2019. https://www.washingtonpost.com/news/food/ wp/2017/12/08/it-was-londons-top-rated-restaurant-just-one- problem-it-didnt-exist/.

2. Butler, O. "I Made My Shed the Top-Rated Restaurant on TripAdvisor." *VICE*, December 6, 2017. https://www.vice.com/ en/article/434gqw/i-made-my-shed-the-top-rated-restaurant-on -tripadvisor.

3. Haugtvedt, C. P., Herr, P. M., and Kardes, F. R., eds. *Handbook of Consumer Psychology*. New York: Lawrence Erlbaum Associates, 2008.

4. Butts, R. "Social Comparison Theory." *Salem Press Encyclopedia*, 2020.

5. Ibid.

6. Ibid.

7. Yarrow, K. *Decoding the New Consumer Mind: How and Why We Shop and Buy*. San Francisco: Jossey-Bass, 2014.

8. Haugtvedt, Herr, and Kardes, eds. *Handbook of Consumer Psychology*.

9. Sevilla, J., and Redden, J. P. "Limited Availability Reduces the Rate of Satiation." *Journal of Marketing Research* 51, no. 2 (2014), 205–217.

10. Amaldoss, W., and Jain, S. "Pricing of Conspicuous Goods: A Competitive Analysis of Social Effects." *Journal of Marketing Research* 42, no. 1 (2005), 30–42. https://journals.sagepub.com/doi/10.1509/jmkr.42.1.30.56883.

11. Roof, K. "Clubhouse Discusses Funding at About $4 Billion Value." Bloomberg.com. April 6, 2021. https://www.bloomberg.com/news/articles/2021-04-06/clubhouse-is-said-to-discuss-funding-at-about-4-billion-value.

12. Amaldoss and Jain. "Pricing of Conspicuous Goods."

13. "Scents and Sensibility." *Marketing Week*, July 3, 1997. https://www.marketingweek.com/scents-and-sensibility/.

14. Kodali, Sucharita. "Digital Go-to-Market Review: Home Goods Brands, 2020," *Forrester Report*, October 1, 2020. https://www.forrester.com/report/Digital-GoToMarket-Review-Home-Goods-Brands-2020/RES161596.

15. Sularia, S. "Council Post: Combating Gray-Market Activities and Protecting Your Brand (Part II): Seven Best Practices." *Forbes*, April 9, 2021. https://www.forbes.com/sites/forbestechcouncil/2021/04/09/combating-gray-market-activities-and-protecting-your-brand-part-ii-seven-best-practices/.

16. Aftab, M. A., Yuanjian, Q., Kabir, N., and Barua, Z. "Super Responsive Supply Chain: The Case of Spanish Fast Fashion Retailer Inditex-Zara." *International Journal of Business and Management* 13, no. 5 (2018), 212. https://doi.org/10.5539/ijbm.v13n5p212.

17. Byun, S., and Sternquist, B. "Here Today, Gone Tomorrow: Consumer Reactions to Perceived Limited Availability." *Journal*

*of Marketing Theory and Practice* 20, no. 2 (2012), 223–234. doi:10.2753/MTP1069-6679200207.

18.  Ton, Z., Corsi, E., and Dessain, V. "ZARA: Managing Stores for Fast Fashion." Case Study. Harvard Business School, November 23, 2009.

19.  Byun and Sternquist. "Here Today, Gone Tomorrow."

20.  "About OdySea Aquarium." OdySea Aquarium. Accessed August 21, 2021. https://www.odyseaaquarium.com/about/.

21.  "OdySea Aquarium in Scottsdale, AZ—the Southwest's Largest Aquarium." OdySea Aquarium. Accessed August 21, 2021. https://www.odyseaaquarium.com/.

22.  Richards, K. "M&M's Made a Magical, Interactive Pop-Up Where Fans Vote for a New Crunchy Chocolate Flavor." *Adweek*, April 20, 2018. https://www.adweek.com/brand-marketing/mms -made-a-magical-interactive-pop-up-where-fans-vote-for-a-new -crunchy-chocolate-flavor/.

23.  Becker, B. "14 Examples of Experiential Marketing Campaigns That'll Give You Serious Event Envy." *HubSpot Blog*, August 16, 2021. https://blog.hubspot.com/marketing/best-experiential-mar-keting-campaigns.

24.  Mars, Incorporated. "M&M's® Announces Crunchy Mint as Winning Flavor in the 2018 'Flavor Vote' Campaign." *PR Newswire*, August 1, 2018. https://www.prnewswire.com/news-releases/mms-announces-crunchy-mint-as-winning-flavor-in-the-2018-flavor-vote-campaign-300689947.html.

25.  Fombelle, P. W., Sirianni, N. J., Goldstein, N. J., and Cialdini, R. B. "Let Them All Eat Cake: Providing VIP Services Without the Cost of Exclusion for Non-VIP Customers." *Journal of Business Research* 68, no. 9 (2015), 1987–1996. doi:10.1016/j.jbusres.2015.01.018.

26.  Ibid.

## Chapter 8

1.  Gralnick, J. "$175,000 Mattress Sold as 'Investment' in Good Sleep." *CNBC*, March 19, 2013. https://www.cnbc.com/id/100563624.

2.  Adams, W. Lee. "The Royal Bed: Is a Good Night's Sleep Worth $175,000?" *Time*, March 21, 2013. https://style.time.com/2013/03/21/the-royal-bed-is-a-good-nights-sleep-worth-175000/.

3.  Bowerman, Mary. "People Are Freaking Out over Starbucks Unicorn Frappuccino." *USA Today*, April 18, 2017. https://www .usatoday.com/story/money/nation-now/2017/04/18/people -freaking-out-over-starbucks-unicorn-frappuccino/100592430/.

4.  Koltun, N. "Mobile Campaign of the Year: Starbucks Unicorn Frappuccino." *Marketing Dive*, December 4, 2017. https://www .marketingdive.com/news/mobile-campaign-of-the-year -starbucks-unicorn-frappuccino/510799/.

5.  Dimon, J. "Starbucks: The Unicorn in the Report." *Seeking Alpha*. May 5, 2017. https://seekingalpha.com/article/4069794-starbucks -unicorn-in-report.

6.  "Korbel Releases Limited-Edition Valentine's Day Bottle." *Beverage Industry*, October 28, 2015. https://www.bevindustry.com/ articles/88205-korbel-releases-limited-edition-valentines-day -bottle.

7.  "History." Panerai. Accessed August 31, 2021. https://www.panerai .com/us/en/about-panerai/history.html.

8.  Yarrow, K. *Decoding the New Consumer Mind: How and Why We Shop and Buy*. San Francisco: Jossey-Bass, 2014.

9.  "History." Panerai.

10. Yarrow. *Decoding the New Consumer Mind*.

11. Ibid.

12. Ibid.

13. Greene, L. "The Paneristi: The Benefits of Engaging with Your Cult Followers." *Financial Times*, September 10, 2010. https:// www.ft.com/content/5715a3d0-bba5-11df-89b6-00144feab49a.

14. "Self-Expression." *Merriam-Webster*. Accessed August 31, 2021. https://www.merriam-webster.com/dictionary/self-expression.

15. Chae, H., Kim, S., Lee, J., and Park, K. "Impact of Product Characteristics of Limited Edition Shoes on Perceived Value, Brand Trust, and Purchase Intention; Focused on the Scarcity Message Frequency." *Journal of Business Research* 120 (November 2020), 398–406. doi:10.1016/j.jbusres.2019.11.040.

16. The quote was obtained from the website Goodreads. Accessed September 2, 2021. https://www.goodreads.com/quotes/187115 -why-fit-in-when-you-were-born-to-stand-out. (*Note:* There is speculation if Dr. Seuss ever used these exact words.)

17. Chae, Kim, Lee, and Park. "Impact of Product Characteristics of Limited Edition Shoes on Perceived Value, Brand Trust, and Purchase Intention."

18. Gierl, H., and Huettl, V. "Are Scarce Products Always More Attractive? The Interaction of Different Types of Scarcity Signals with Products' Suitability for Conspicuous Consumption." *International Journal of Research in Marketing* 27, no. 3 (2010), 225–235. doi:10.1016/j.ijresmar.2010.02.002.

19. Veblen, T. *The Theory of the Leisure Class*. Project Gutenberg, March 1, 1997. https://www.gutenberg.org/ebooks/833.

20. "Leisure Class." Encyclopedia.com, June 8, 2008. https://www.encyclopedia.com/social-sciences-and-law/sociology-and-social-reform/sociology-general-terms-and-concepts/leisure-class.

21. Gierl and Huettl. "Are Scarce Products Always More Attractive?"

22. Bagwell, L. S., and Bernheim, B. D. "Veblen Effects in a Theory of Conspicuous Consumption." *American Economic Review* 86, no. 3 (1996), 349–373.

23. Wu, L., and Lee, C. "Limited Edition for Me and Best Seller for You: The Impact of Scarcity Versus Popularity Cues on Self Versus Other-Purchase Behavior." *Journal of Retailing* 92, no. 4 (2016), 486–499. doi:10.1016/j.jretai.2016.08.001.

24. Bagwell and Bernheim. "Veblen Effects in a Theory of Conspicuous Consumption."

25. Dörnyei, K. R. "Limited Edition Packaging: Objectives, Implementations and Related Marketing Mix Decisions of a Scarcity Product Tactic." *Journal of Consumer Marketing* 37, no. 6 (2020), 617–627.

26. Stein, J. "Chaos Day Is Coming." *Paste Magazine*, January 11, 2017. https://www.pastemagazine.com/drink/the-ram-/chaos-day-is-coming/.

27. "Would You Drive 1,200 Miles to Get Your Hands on This Beer? There's Nothing like Scarcity—Real or Perceived—to Boost Demand, Which Is Why the Hottest Thing at Craft Breweries Today Is Limited-Edition Beers." *Crain's Chicago Business*, February 10, 2017.

28. Bromwich, J. E. "We Asked: Why Does Oreo Keep Releasing New Flavors?" *New York Times*, December 16, 2020. https://www.nytimes.com/2020/12/16/style/oreo-flavors.html.

29. Ibid.

30. Struble, C. "Captain Marvel Inspired Recipes: Powering the Hero Within Everyone." *FoodSided*, March 1, 2019. https://foodsided.com/2019/03/01/captain-marvel-inspired-recipes-powering-hero-within-everyone/.

## Chapter 9

1. Kristofferson, K., McFerran, B., Morales, A. C., and Dahl, D.W. "The Dark Side of Scarcity Promotions: How Exposure to Limited-Quantity Promotions Can Induce Aggression." *Journal of Consumer Research* 43, no. 5 (2017), 683–706. https://doi.org/10.1093/jcr/ucw056.

2.  Cialdini, R. B., and Rhoads, K. V. L. "Human Behavior and the Marketplace." *Marketing Research* 13, no. 3 (2001), 8–13.

3.  Lee, S. M., Ryu, G., and Chun, S. "Perceived Control and Scarcity Appeals." *Social Behavior and Personality* 46, no. 3 (2018), 361–374. https://doi.org/10.2224/sbp.6367.

4.  Roy, R. "The Effects of Envy on Scarcity Appeals in Advertising: Moderating Role of Product Involvement." *Advances in Consumer Research* 44, no. 756 (2016).

5.  Aguirre-Rodriguez, A. "The Effect of Consumer Persuasion Knowledge on Scarcity Appeal Persuasiveness." *Journal of Advertising* 42, no. 4 (2013), 371–379. https://doi.org/10.1080/00913367.2013.803186.

6.  Lee, S. Y., and Jung, S. "Shelf-Based Scarcity and Consumers' Product Choice: The Role of Scarcity Disconfirmation." *Social Behavior and Personality* 47, no. 5 (2019), 1–10. https://doi.org/10.2224/sbp.7957.

7.  van Herpen, E., Pieters, F. G. M., and Zeelenberg, M. "How Product Scarcity Impacts on Choice: Snob and Bandwagon Effects." *Advances in Consumer Research* 32 (2005), 623–624.

8.  Lee and Jung. "Shelf-Based Scarcity and Consumers' Product Choice."

9.  Niesiobędzka, M. "An Experimental Study of the Bandwagon Effect in Conspicuous Consumption." *Current Issues in Personality Psychology* 6, no. 1 (2018), 26–33. https://doi.org/10.5114/cipp.2017.67896.

10. Lee and Jung. "Shelf-Based Scarcity and Consumers' Product Choice."

11. Thrane, C., and Haugom, E. "Peer Effects on Restaurant Tipping in Norway: An Experimental Approach." *Journal of Economic Behavior & Organization* 176 (August 2020), 244–252. doi:10.1016/j.jebo.2020.04.010.

12. Cai, H., Chen, Y., and Fang, H. "Observational Learning: Evidence from a Randomized Natural Field Experiment." *American Economic Review* 99, no. 3 (2009).

13. Smith, G. "QVC's Plan to Survive Amazon Might Actually Be Working." *Bloomberg*, February 6, 2018. https://www.bloomberg.com/news/features/2018-02-06/qvc-s-plan-to-survive-amazon-and-escape-the-cable-tv-death-spiral.

14. Ibid.

15. Gierl, H., Plantsch, M., and Schweidler, J. "Scarcity Effects on Sales Volume in Retail." *International Review of Retail,*

*Distribution & Consumer Research* 18, no. 1 (2008), 45–61. https://psycnet.apa.org/record/2008-01217-003.

16. Cremer, S., and Loebbecke, C. "Selling Goods on E-Commerce Platforms: The Impact of Scarcity Messages." *Electronic Commerce Research and Applications* 47 (2021), 101039. https://doi.org/10.1016/j.elerap.2021.101039.

17. Cialdini, R. B. *Influence, New and Expanded: The Psychology of Persuasion.* New York: HarperCollins Publishers, 2021.

18. Daspin, E. "The T-Shirt You Can't Get." *Wall Street Journal*, October 10, 2003. https://www.wsj.com/articles/SB10657460 791372700.

19. LeVick, K. "Behind the Label: Robinhood." *TheStreet*, August 6, 2021. https://www.thestreet.com/investing/behind-label-robinhood.

## Chapter 10

1. Stump, S. "Oscar Mayer Comes Out with Bologna-Inspired Sheet Masks." TODAY.com, January 19, 2022. https://www.today.com/food/trends/oscar-mayer-comes-bologna-inspired-skincare-masks-rcna12728.

2. Tyko, K. "Oscar Mayer Sells Out of Bologna-Inspired Face Masks on Amazon, Plans to Restock." *USA Today*, January 19, 2022. https://www.usatoday.com/story/money/shopping/2022/01/19/oscar-mayer-bologna-masks-amazon/6563703001/.

# Acknowledgments

Writing a book is no easy feat and one that would not be possible without outside help and support. Where do I even start with my gratitude?

I am especially thankful to my literary agent, Cynthia Zigmund, who helped transform my idea into reality. She spent hours upon hours helping me flesh out my thoughts and gave incredible feedback along the way. Cynthia patiently answered the random questions that would pop up in my mind and provided amazing advice. Cynthia, this book wouldn't have come to fruition without you.

Now, to the editorial team at McGraw Hill, especially Cheryl Segura. From the moment we had our first conversation via Zoom, I knew she was someone I wanted to work with. Cheryl made the entire editing process enjoyable and had so much great input. Page by page, Cheryl transformed the book into something great. And how could I not love our dialogue on the scarcity we experienced in our everyday lives? I am incredibly grateful for you, Cheryl.

When I started on this book, I knew that I wanted to not just explain scarcity in theory, but also show it in practice. What better way than to give firsthand accounts from successful people in business? I was blown away at how generous my interviewees were with their time and knowledge. Thank you to Kevin Harrington, Jim McCann, Dean Barrett, Levi Conlow, David Cogan, Melinda Spigel, and Dr. Jeremy Nicholson. Your stories brought the information in this book to life. Plus, with each interview, I felt that I personally learned something new. I am very appreciative of all of you.

And thank you to Dr. Robert Cialdini, for reviewing my manuscript and for all his kind words. I thoroughly respect and admire your work and have enjoyed our conversations.

A special thanks to Dr. Randy Gibb and Dr. Allison Mason at Grand Canyon University, who were supportive of me as I continued to work on this book. You were both very encouraging, and I appreciate you sharing in my enthusiasm and excitement.

Finally, I am grateful for my husband, Mike. I lost track of how many days and nights I bombarded him with my latest thoughts on scarcity and the book in general. He was always patient and listened to me ramble on. I owe you, Mike.

# Index

low acceptance rates of,
26
Scott (interviewee), 91–92
seat reservation process, at
Eliances, 134
self-expression, 147–148,
151–152, 161
self-respect, pursuit of, 153
Seoul Mamas, 181–182
service bundles, 155–156
service-oriented businesses, 178
*Sex and the City* (TV show),
31–32
Shamrock Shake, 101–102
*Shark Tank* (TV show), xv, 12
The Shed at Dulwich,
123–124
shelf space, shopper decisions
and, 168–169
shopping channel example,
173–174
short renewal cycle, of fast
fashion stores, 75,
138–139
simplicity, of flash sale, 112, 121
Singer, William "Rick," 25–26
*Sixty Minutes* (TV show), 25
slogans, 97
sneakerheads, 169
social acceptance, 167
social comparison theory,
126–127
social cues, time-related
scarcity and, 121
social media
brands coupons and, 115
as reference group, 151
self-expression and, 151

Unicorn Frappuccino and,
147
social need, to be envied, 153
social psychology, 12
Sony, 132
South African cruise, 71–72
spa, in South Africa, 77–78
special collections, of grocery
stores, 139–140
special-edition Oreos, 156
Spigel, Melinda, 70
Stacey (interviewee), 58–59
staffing, of the Shed at
Dulwich, 125
Stallone, Sylvester, 149
standing out, 31
Star Wars ride, at Hollywood
Studios, 33–35
Starbucks, 107–108
steak house, 119
Stewart, Kristin, 65
store coupons, 116–117
stories
backpack, 91–92
grocery store, 35–36, 175
about scarcity experiences,
183–184
wine shop, 43
stress, 104, 121
strong argument, in cinnamon
twist study, 53
studies, 14
Campbell's soup, 36–37,
48–49
candy, 128–129
cinnamon twist, 52–53
closing time effect, 37–38
coupon, 115–116
cruise traveler, 71–72

# About the Author

MINDY WEINSTEIN, PhD, IS one of the leading experts in marketing and has been named one of the top women in digital marketing globally. She has gained a reputation for writing and speaking about influence and has presented to both domestic and international audiences.

Mindy teaches and leads marketing courses at Grand Canyon University, University of Denver, The Wharton School of the University of Pennsylvania, and Columbia Business School. She's been featured on Fox, NBC, Bloomberg Radio, and ABC, and has been quoted as an expert in the *Huffington Post*, the *Washington Post*, and the *Arizona Republic*.

Mindy has a unique combination of practical and academic experience. She began her career as a copywriter for a business-to-business training company and later moved into the personal finance industry. The Great Recession of 2008 completely changed and catapulted her platform when she decided to try a new career in website content writing and took her first step into the world of digital marketing. In this role, she worked with and trained organizations including Facebook, The Weather Channel, Kijiji (an eBay-owned company), World Fuel Services, Hampton Products, and more.

As a marketer, Mindy has always had an interest in psychology, leading her to pursue a PhD in general psychology with an emphasis in technology. She spent years researching and writing about scarcity from an academic perspective. However, she also realized the power of this influence principle and began applying it in her own life. Mindy has secured many clients and customers using what she knows about scarcity and is often able to convince her husband and boys to take on household chores they wouldn't have otherwise done!

Visit mindyweinstein.com to learn more.